KT-394-661

C o n t e n t s

KEY TO MAPS

✈ Airport	🏛 Museum
✝ Church	✚ Hospital
⤬⤬⤬ Railway line	④ Road number
✉ Post office	♪ Public telephone
Ⓢ Bank	═══ Motorway
𝒊 Information	🚌 Bus station

Introduction

Cuba has come a long way in the last 15 years. The country is transforming itself from an old-fashioned, inefficient and slightly downmarket destination for travellers to one that has attractive facilities, robust infrastructure and an attitude to service and efficiency that makes visiting Cuba a pleasurable and exciting experience. According to travel experts it is now one of the 'hot' countries to visit.

It is not hard to understand why: beautiful white beaches with crystal-clear waters attract package holiday-makers and water sports enthusiasts alike; Havana is regaining its former splendour, with systematic restoration of the Old City; Cuban music is wildly popular in many countries, resulting in many travellers visiting the country just for the nightlife and salsa dancing; and nature lovers are increasingly drawn to the richness of flora, fauna, unspoilt countryside and spectacular marine life of the island.

Managing one's expectations is the first challenge that a visitor will have to face when planning a visit. Any number of viewings of *The Buena Vista Social Club*, documentaries about the Cuban Revolution, or listening to Cuban salsa music will not prepare you for the experience of being in Cuba. It is like no country you have ever visited, so do not expect an archetypally Caribbean island or a typical Latin American country, for it is neither.

Many visitors to Cuba tend to come on package holidays, and only ever get to see the all-inclusive beach resort in which they are staying, as well as a day or two in the capital, Havana. This is a great shame, because Cuba has so much more to offer, and visitors just need a small injection of confidence to look beyond the clichés and experience the real Cuba.

There are delightful colonial towns to visit such as Trinidad, there are tranquil and rich natural habitats to visit such as the Península de Zapata, and there are more beaches and top-notch diving spots than you can shake a stick at. Cuba can cater to many tastes; you just need a bit of planning, an open mind and a thirst for adventure that will reap great rewards in your time on the island.

In these days of globalisation and runaway capitalism, Cuba is one of the few countries in the western hemisphere that has the capacity to challenge one's deepest assumptions about governance, money, family, freedom and happiness in general. Its contradictions are many. How can a communist country be so good at attracting foreign package holiday-makers? How can Havana still be so beautiful even after more than 40 years of neglect? How can a country so poor have such a healthy and educated population? How have this country's ideals and culture survived this long at the doorstep of the world's biggest capitalist superpower? The questions will keep coming to you long after you have left the country. Like many of us, you are likely to feel a mixture of perplexity, admiration and warmth for this large, isolated island in the middle of the sun-kissed Caribbean Sea.

Street performers in Havana Vieja

Land and economy

Known as the key to the Gulf, Cuba is the largest of the West Indies and one of the largest islands in the world. Shaped rather like a crocodile, it is a long, narrow island in the westernmost part of the insular Caribbean, at the entrance of the Gulf of Mexico.

Cuban boy assembling a go-cart

The land

The island is 1,200km (746 miles) long and reaches 210km (130 miles) at its widest point. The Cuban archipelago comprises an area of 110,992sq km (42,850 sq miles) and has more than 300 natural beaches of fine white sand lapped by crystal-clear waters, the most famous being Varadero. Cuba has a wide variety of landscapes, ranging from plains to hilly and mountainous areas. The three most important mountain ranges are Cordillera de Guaniguanico, in the western part of the country, Escambray in the centre, and Sierra Maestra in the east, with Turquino peak, the highest point in the country, at 1,974m (6,476ft) above sea level. The rest of the territory is plain and fertile. There are plenty of caves, some of outstanding beauty, such as Bellamar in Matanzas province.

Most rivers in Cuba are relatively short and the water currents are quite strong. They flow through the mountains, creating beautiful waterfalls such as Salto del Caburní and Agabama Falls. Cuba's longest river is Cauto, (about 240km, or 150 miles long) located in the east. There are also many reservoirs and lakes. In rural areas, lush natural settings make for spectacular scenery, and migratory routes for birdlife can be seen in the countryside. Rural life operates in different ways and confers its own unique characteristics on the Cuban countryside.

Urban areas contain 75 per cent of the population, while the remainder lives in the countryside. On the whole, Cuban towns contain a wide mix of architectural styles, although many buildings are run-down. However, in some cities' old quarters, for example, Havana or Trinidad, a colonial ambience has been preserved.

Flora and Fauna

Cuba's flora and fauna are very rich and diverse. There are more than 300 protected areas that cover approximately

Tobacco farming near Viñales

22 per cent of the national territory, and the country has six areas that have been declared Biosphere Reserves by UNESCO: Guanahacabibes Peninsula, Sierra del Rosario and Ciénaga de Zapata National Park, in the west; El Caguanes National Park in the centre; and Baconao Park and Cuchillas del Toa in the east. More than 50 per cent of Cuba's flora is endemic and its variety is illustrated by the fact that Cuba holds 4 per cent of the total flora on the planet. Most appealing among these are orchids, cacti and the palm tree.

Endemic species are also much in evidence when it comes to amphibians and reptiles. The crocodile, commonly found in crocodile breeding centres in the country, is very characteristic of Cuba. Around 400 species of birds are estimated to exist in Cuba, and the country still preserves rare species like the *zunzuncito* which is the smallest bird in the world, as well as the tiniest frog, a very small bat called Mariposa and a scorpion no longer than 14mm ($^1/_2$ inch).

National symbols

The national flower is the butterfly lily (a type of white-coloured jasmine that is exquisitely perfumed), while the bird is the Trogan bird (a native species whose plumage contains the same colours as the Cuban flag). The Royal Palm is the national tree and is found in abundance throughout the island.

The economy

The Cuban economy is a centralised system, dependent on two main industries: tourism and sugar. The sugar industry has been the dominant industry for all but the last 15 years, and the country is gradually lessening its dependence on sugar exports as a source of revenue. Tourism is now growing rapidly, following the government's targeting of this industry for growth since the 1990s. There has been massive foreign investment, particularly from Canadian, Spanish and other European corporations, especially along the Varadero coast, in order to attract package holiday-makers. As a result, visitor numbers are forecast to rise from 3 million in 2004 to 7 million in 2010.

Other major sectors of the economy include tobacco, coffee, rum, honey, cocoa and citrus fruits. Cuba is also a world leader in research and exports in the pharmaceutical and biotechnological industries. Other industries include those for construction materials, fishing, nickel mining (the country holds the largest open-face reserves in the world), copper, magnesium and refractory chrome.

A final but important source of revenue for the country is the sending of money from Cuban émigrés, mostly now living in Florida, to their families in Cuba.

The butterfly lily – the national flower

History

The recorded history of Cuba begins with the arrival of Christopher Columbus on October 28, 1492. Before this, Cuba is thought to have been inhabited by three Amerindian ethnic groups. The Guanajatabey were gatherers who lived in caves; next came the Siboney who were hunters and fishermen; and lastly the Taíno, who came from present-day Venezuela and were the most advanced of the three groups.

American troops entering Havana, 1902

Columbus landed in Cuba during his first voyage of discovery in the New World. He was disappointed not to find gold but was intrigued by the Amerindian practice of puffing at burning rolls of leaves which they called *tobacos*. The island was quickly conquered by the Spanish, mainly due to the relative lack of resistance put up by the Indians, with the exception of chief Hatuey, who was burnt at the stake. Key in this conquest was Diego de Velázquez who completed the annexation of the island to Spain in 1514, and set up several towns (*villas*), including Havana.

The native Indian population was decimated by a combination of forced labour, cruelty, and European viruses, which they were completely unable to cope with. Because of this, by 1526 the Spanish had to start importing slaves from Africa.

Cuba was used by the Spanish as a port of call for ships taking riches from the New World back to Spain, and as a strategic military base for their colonies. By the 16th century, this wealth

A slave-driven coffee grinder from colonial times

attracted the attention of pirates, buccaneers and corsairs, the latter sanctioned by Britain, France and the Netherlands. This led to the building of impressive fortifications around the main ports of Cuba, including Havana.

Sugar cane and tobacco began to be cultivated on a large scale and were traded solely with Spain. Havana was briefly occupied by the British in 1762, but they left the following year as a result of the Treaty of Paris, in exchange for Florida. One of the results of this brief occupation was that Cuban landowners began to realise that trading with other countries besides

Spain was a more economically attractive proposition.

By the end of the 18th century, Cuba was a plantation society with a Creole aristocracy, Cuban-born people of Spanish descent who soon established a Cuban national identity. Nationalist revolts were put down by the Spanish, but the newly-emerged Creole middle class were determined to gain independence for their country from the Spanish crown.

On October 10, 1868, Carlos Manuel de Céspedes, a Creole landowner, freed his slaves, triggering the first Cuban war of independence. This Ten Years War ended in 1878 with the Convention of Zanjón, which was rejected by some revolutionaries, including the famous General Antonio Maceo, Máximo Gómez and de Céspedes himself. War resumed in 1895, with José Martí, a Cuban intellectual, at the forefront of the struggle. In the meantime, the USA was becoming concerned about the substantial investments that it had been building up in Cuba, especially in the form of sugar plantations and mills. The explosion of the US battleship *Maine* in Havana harbour in February 1898 was the excuse that the USA needed for declaring war on Spain. The US Navy defeated the Spanish fleet and the Treaty of Paris was subsequently signed between the USA and Spain, which ignored Cuban interests. Cuban nationalists realised that they were at last free from their Spanish colonial masters, but were under US military occupation for the next four years, and under US 'supervision' for the next 30 or so years.

Formal independence was granted to Cuba on May 20, 1902, but the new Republic was constrained by the Platt Amendment, passed by US Congress, which enabled the USA to retain its naval bases, including the one in Guantánamo Bay, and reserved the right to intervene in Cuban domestic affairs. Cuba was essentially dependent on the USA for trade, there were huge social inequalities, and the majority of rural people suffered grinding poverty. As a result, resentment against the USA for its political and economic domination of the island was to prove one of the driving forces behind the Cuban Revolution in the 1950s.

From 1924 to 1933 Cuba was ruled by Gerardo Machado, a dictator who oversaw a period of tyranny, political corruption and strikes. Sergeant Fulgencio Batista became a key figure in the ensuing years, heading a revolt of army officers and placing several presidential puppets, before holding power himself in the years 1933–44. A series of presidents followed, but they failed to halt the corruption, political violence and public discontent. On June 1, 1952, Batista staged a military coup, and ruled Cuba with violent repression of mostly student demonstrations, and a disdain for the common Cuban who became ever poorer. Batista was backed by the Americans, and turned Cuba into a glamorous 'pleasure island', with prostitution, gambling and a sensual tropical life that attracted American businessmen, film stars and Mafiosi. It was this state of affairs that was to lead to the Cuban Revolution.

The Cuban revolution

The importance of the Cuban Revolution in the history of the island cannot be underestimated. It changed everything: not only the political ideology and government of Cuba, but its culture, economy, international relations, national identity and ideals, which have remained virtually unchanged for over 45 years.

The Cuban Revolution effectively began with Batista's coup in 1952, which led to the denouncement of his new government by Fidel Castro Ruz, an active student leader. This found support from a large number of ordinary Cubans, but peaceful protests had little effect. Castro and his close associates decided to turn to violent means to achieve their aims, starting with the unsuccessful raid on the Moncada army barracks in Santiago de Cuba. Many were captured and executed, but Castro and several others escaped. Castro's life was saved by the army officer who captured him, who recognised him from their student days and decided not to take him back to Santiago de Cuba to face certain torture and death. Castro and others, including his brother Raúl, were imprisoned on the Isla de la Juventud but only served two years before being granted amnesty. Castro's defence speech during the trial was to become the basis of a reform programme and a summary of his revolutionary thinking, named after the famous last sentence: 'History will absolve me'.

After a period in exile in Mexico where he met Che Guevara, Castro set up the '26 July Movement' and formed a band of 82 revolutionaries. They sailed on the yacht *Granma* to the eastern tip of Cuba on December 2, 1956, and, after being surprised by Batista's troops, escaped to the Sierra Maestra mountains. There, they rallied support and trained an army of guerillas, launching attacks on government troops and taking their supplies and weapons. Popular support was greatly strengthened by the setting up of a guerilla radio station *Radio Rebelde*, which was avidly listened to all over the island. The growing numbers of *barbudos* ('bearded men', so called because they all grew beards during their time in the mountains) were joined by a mixture of students, farmers, army deserters and city men recruited by the urban branch of the 'Movimiento 26 de Julio'.

The fighting reached its peak in 1958 when two columns of guerillas marched through the island, one led by Che Guevara and Camilo Cienfuegos which headed west to the centre of the island, and the other led by Raúl Castro which headed towards Guantánamo. The Battle of Santa Clara was decisive: Che Guevara's troops overcame government forces against overwhelming odds, and captured a troop train laden with supplies and armaments. As a result, Batista fled Cuba on December 31,

1958, and victory was declared for the revolution. On January 1, 1959, Che Guevara and Camilo Cienfuegos entered Havana in triumph, while Castro did the same in Santiago de Cuba.

Manuel Urrutia was initially elected president upon Batista's escape, but by February 16 Fidel Castro was persuaded to take office after initially refusing, and was elected prime minister.

Fidel Castro and his troops, 1956

Economic isolation

The Cuban Revolution which took control of the island in 1959 was the catalyst for hostility from the USA, leading to economic sanctions which have had a profound effect on the economy of Cuba.

From 1960 onwards, Fidel Castro led Cuba down the path to socialism in the face of huge pressure from the USA, which only had the effect of hardening the leftward leanings of the regime. All foreign banks, sugar and oil refineries, foreign-owned companies and private property were nationalised and taken under the control of the state. The USA lost its substantial economic assets, and the US mafia lost its money-laundering operations, including gambling, prostitution, hotels and nightclubs.

Following the unsuccessful Bay of Pigs invasion in 1961, Fidel Castro declared that Cuba was socialist, and established mutual benefit treaties and strong relations with the USSR, China and North Korea. The USA responded by severing diplomatic relations with Cuba and installing a full trade embargo, as well as putting pressure on other Latin American countries to do likewise.

The effect soon began to be felt, with rationing imposed in March 1962 which continues even today. Cuba became more economically dependent on the USSR, relying on favourable trade terms for oil, and receiving millions in economic aid, machinery and technicians, equivalent to 25 per cent of Cuba's wealth. By the 1980s, living

standards for Cubans still had not improved and further austerity was experienced with the Latin American debt crisis.

The collapse of the communist system in the USSR by the early 1990s signalled a change in the government's economic policy, and Castro realised the necessity of gaining foreign earnings in the face of the cessation of aid and economic assistance from the USSR. A programme of economic liberalisation ensued, with farmers' markets being allowed to operate. Tourism has become a priority in Cuba's economic policy, and a large amount of joint ventures have been signed with foreign companies, especially in the tourist and travel sectors, allowing much-needed investment in the country.

While rationing still continues, there are private markets for food where goods are paid for in US dollars, and an active black market. One growing social problem as a result of Cuba's economic isolation is the widening income gap between those who earn dollars in the tourist industry and the majority who don't. For example, Cubans who rent rooms in their *casas particulares* generate a relatively attractive income, even after paying the high government taxes for holding the relevant licence. Because the majority of the population earn Cuban pesos, and most consumer goods are sold in US dollars, this makes many products way out of reach of most ordinary Cubans. As a result, some Cubans will do practically anything to earn US dollars from tourists.

To give an example of the current rationing system, the average Cuban adult will be allowed to buy five eggs per month, 3kg (6.5lb) of rice, and various quantities of other produce including beans, sugar and salt. Cubans have ration books which allow them to buy these amounts of produce at low national prices. Anything over and above this is available in private markets at much higher prices. The availability of non-staple foods varies each month according to harvests. Rations do give some help, but they are by no means sufficient for someone to live on.

Cuba is diversifying its economy, especially in agriculture, in order to reduce its dependence on imported foreign food. The gradual move to a more unstructured economy that allows private enterprise will inevitably lead to 'growing pains' as the country adapts. In the meantime, however, there is no sign that the US trade embargo will be relaxed. This is mainly because of the importance of Florida, and especially Miami, to any US presidential candidate, a state with a large and vocal anti-Castro, Cuban émigré population, who are vehemently opposed to the relaxation of the trade embargo.

Facing page: horse-drawn cart fitted with lorry wheels

History timeline

1492	Cuba discovered by Christopher Colombus (Cristóbal Colón in Spanish) on his first voyage. He claims the island for Spain.
1514	The annexation of Cuba is completed by the Spanish under Diego de Velázquez.
1519	The city of San Cristóbal de La Habana is founded on the site of present-day Havana.
1526	The Spanish begin the importation of slaves from Africa.
1555	Havana is sacked by the Frenchman Jacques de Sores, leading to the construction of extensive fortifications at Cuban ports, and Havana is established as the gathering point of all Spanish colonial fleets.
1762	English forces occupy Havana and leave the following year after the Treaty of Paris.
1793	Commerce with the USA is formally established although unofficial links are already in place.
1820	The Spanish constitutional regime is re-established, leading to pro-independence pressures, led by priest Félix Varela.
1837	The first railroad in Cuba, the third in the world, is built to support the booming sugar industry.
1868	Carlos Manuel de Céspedes, a Creole landowner, frees his slaves, triggering the first Cuban War of Independence (also known as the Ten Years War).
1878	The Ten Years War ends with the Convention of Zanjón. This is rejected by some revolutionaries, including General Antonio Maceo. This is known as the protest of Baraguá.
1880	Slavery is formally abolished, although its practice only ceases six years later.
1892	The Cuban Revolutionary Party is founded by José Martí as part of the struggle for Cuban independence.

1895	The last War of Independence against Spanish colonial rule begins, and José Martí dies in combat.
1896	Antonio Maceo dies fighting the Spanish.
1898	The explosion of the US battleship *Maine* in Havana harbour leads to American intervention in the War of Independence, and the defeat of the Spanish navy.
1902	Cuba achieves independence but is supervised by the USA as a neo-colonial republic.
1906	US Marines occupy Cuba for a second time under the provision of the Platt Amendment, signed by US Congress.
1925	The Communist Cuban Party of Cuba is founded by Carlos Baliño.
1933	US-backed dictator Gerardo Machado forced to resign after ten years in power.
1940	A democratic and liberal constitution put into force.
1952	Army general Fulgencio Batista stages a military

	coup and suspends the constitution.
1953	Revolutionaries headed by Fidel Castro stage a failed assault on the Moncada Garrison.
1956	Castro, Che Guevara and 82 revolutionaries resume the struggle.
1959	The Revolution triumphs after Batista flees Cuba.
1961	US-backed Cuban exiles launch a failed invasion at the Bay of Pigs.
1962	The USSR removes its missiles from Cuban soil.
1976	The Constitution of the Republic of Cuba put into effect with elections to the National Assembly.
1982	Havana declared a World Heritage Site by UNESCO.
1998	Pope John Paul II visits Cuba.
2002	US Naval base at Guantánamo Bay used to intern al-Qaeda and Taliban prisoners.
2005	Cuba is hit by a series of hurricanes in one of the worst seasons on record.

Governance

Although the Castro regime is seen as severe and liable to periodic crackdowns on dissidents, it is still popular and there is a tangible sense of national pride among the population. Much of this is due to the continued economic embargo by the USA, which has hardened Cuba's determination to maintain its socialist values and has kept Castro firmly in power for the last 40-odd years.

The crest of Cuba

The political system

Cuba is a communist republic with a centrally planned economy. The present Constitution of the Republic of Cuba was approved by 98 per cent of legal voters. The supreme government body is the National Assembly of the People's Power, which appoints the State Council, the Council of Ministers and the president of the State Council, who is Head of State and Government (currently Fidel Castro).

There are 589 members of the National Assembly of the People's Power, who are elected by universal suffrage every five years. Below the

National Assembly are the Provincial and Municipal Assemblies which are elected in the same way, every two and a half years. It is primarily through the delegates in these assemblies that the people express their wishes.

The only political party is the Cuban Communist Party, and citizens directly elect candidates, as the Party itself cannot legally propose its candidates. Decision-making is done by the National Assembly which passes all laws, based on the 'advice' of the President. It is called a democratic process, based on the ideal of 'the right of the people to eat, to be educated and to be treated in hospitals'. However, the National Assembly does not have the power to remove the President.

A common political slogan, meaning, 'Until victory. Always.'

Administrative districts

The island has 14 provinces plus the special municipality of the Isla de la Juventud. For economic, political and administrative purposes, Cuba is divided into 169 municipalities, of which the capitals are as follows: Santiago de Cuba, Holguín, Guantánamo, Bayamo, Las Tunas, Camagüey, Ciego de Avila, Sancti-Spíritus, Santa Clara, Cienfuegos,

Matanzas, Pinar del Río and Havana (the latter being two provinces).

More flexibility

In 1992 various amendments were introduced to the Cuban Constitution, among them the guaranteeing of foreign investments, more flexibility in foreign trade, and the introduction of direct election by universal suffrage of deputies to the National Assembly. This relaxation of socialist principles forms part of a more pragmatic approach by the Cuban government, which realised the urgent need for foreign investment and foreign earnings, in the wake of the disintegration of the Soviet Union, its most important ally.

Political theory

The theory behind Cuba's political system is based on the ideals of the Communist Party, which works for the interests of the working class, and whose aim is to achieve a society in which everyone is equal, has the same rights, and can fulfil their dreams in a collective way. The important distinction between this and the capitalist path is that here, the collective is more important than the individual. This concept is difficult for many visitors to understand and is the cause of much frustration among ambitious and liberal Cubans. The other important strand in Cuba's political ideals is the thinking of José Martí, whose ideals of freedom, happiness and independence continue to inspire Cubans today.

Achievements of the Revolution

The political system has underpinned several important achievements.

Education in Cuba is free and compulsory up to the 9th grade (age 14–15) of schooling. In 1961 Cuba carried out a national campaign against illiteracy, and today in Cuba every adult citizen knows how to read and write. There are teaching polytechnics and specialised institutes in all provinces, and also a number of universities.

Cuba's system of primary health care covers the entire country and is considered to be unique in Latin America. Health services are free for all Cubans. The infant mortality rate is 7.1 per thousand live births, and life expectancy at birth is 75.2 years, figures that are better than many developed countries. Cuban medicine is very advanced, powered by the many scientific research and production companies in the country. Cuba was among the first countries to produce interferon, and its vaccines against Meningitis B and C, and Hepatitis B, are unique in the world. Moreover, the country is one of the world's leading exporters of pharmaceuticals.

Current political issues

The question that has been on many people's lips is what will happen when Castro dies. Many experts say that a succession plan is already in place, in order to maintain political stability in the face of expected US-led pressure to change the communist political system. Raúl Castro seems the most likely candidate to succeed his older brother, although other candidates include the head of the National Assembly, Ricardo Alarcón.

Fidel Castro Ruz has been the dominant figure in Cuban history for the past 40 or so years. In 1959 he was the youngest ruler, and he is now the longest serving head of state in the world. Despite hundreds of assassination attempts since the 1960s, he has seen eight US presidents come and go, and has only recently shown signs of frailty. Castro has personified the Cuban state for decades: as Alejo Carpentier wrote, 'he accomplished what José Martí had promised'.

Many tourists come to Cuba because they want to see the country 'before Castro dies'. The uncertainty about what

several others escaped, later to be caught and imprisoned on the Isla de la Juventud. Castro's defence speech during the trial was to become the basis of a reform programme and a summary of Castro's revolutionary thinking, named after the famous last sentence: 'History will absolve me'.

After imprisonment and then exile, he launched his second armed uprising in 1956, landing in Cuba on the now legendary *Granma* cabin cruiser. Although the uprising was crushed, Castro, along with his brother Raúl and Che Guevara, escaped into the Sierra Maestra mountains where they gradually built up popular support and began guerilla warfare against the US-backed dictatorship of Batista. By 1959, a general revolt had succeeded in overthrowing the dictatorship. After initially declining office, Castro became supreme *commandante*, president and all-round *jefe* (chief), a post that he has held for more than half his life.

His once-famous four-hour speeches and cigar smoking have ended, and rumours of heart problems and arthritis persist. Yet he has always said that he wants his ideals to outlive him: 'Men pass away, people stay; men pass away, ideas live on.'

will happen when he does go only illustrates the all-encompassing effect he has on Cuban political life. Cubans simply refer to him as 'Fidel' in reverential tones.

Born in Mayarí in eastern Cuba on August 13, 1926, his father was originally from Galicia in Spain, and the young Fidel studied with the Jesuits before taking a degree in law. After realising that peaceful protest would not bring about change, he took up the revolutionary cause, and was one of 150 insurgents who attempted to storm the Moncada Barracks in 1953. Many were captured and executed, but Castro and

Facing page: a government sponsored political rally in Havana
This page: Castro and his revolutionaries

People and religion

The population of Cuba is over 11.3 million inhabitants, and over 76 per cent live in urban areas. Population density is 102 inhabitants per square km ($^1/_3$ square mile) and the most densely populated provinces are the City of Havana with a population of 2.2 million, Santiago de Cuba with 1 million and Holguín with roughly the same.

Dancer interpreting the deity of thunder, war and the drum – Shangó

The people of Cuba are culturally mixed, resulting from the intermingling of white Europeans (especially Spanish), blacks descended from African slaves, and Asians descended from the Chinese community. It is estimated that over half of all Cubans are *mulattos*, from mixed races. Cubans are generally very sociable, talkative and outgoing, with a love of laughter and having fun.

There is no real boundary between the home and the street, with many house doors remaining open and much socialising in the street or on balconies. Many people spend the whole day outside, chatting, playing dominoes, flirting or just sitting watching the world go by. The family plays a central role in the lives of most Cubans, with much socialising in the evenings, watching TV or sitting in rocking chairs and talking.

Music plays an important part in people's lives, and little excuse is needed to dance and start a party. One of the most important celebrations is the debut of 15-year-olds in society, when the girls dress up in white dresses.

Cuban society is altering rapidly because of the changing economic landscape and increasing exposure to the outside world. A new middle class is emerging, who earn US dollars in the tourist sector and who can afford many of the 'luxuries' out of reach of most Cubans. This has led to some jealousy and resentment, which is to be expected where neighbourhoods are close and everyone knows everyone else's business. While there is a relatively even distribution of wealth, with no extremes at either end, this is being put under strain by the dollar economy, fuelled by increasing numbers of tourists who bring with them a taste of the outside world that seems so exotic and attractive to many Cubans. Castro is attempting to battle the power of the American dollar.

Batá drums played by the Yoruba Andabo Orchestra

Cubans in the carnival spirit

Following the establishment of tighter trade sanctions by the US, he stripped the US dollar of its legal tender status. This still hasn't stopped some locals from hustling for the occasional tourist buck though.

Religion

Officially, Catholicism is the most widespread religion, although Afro-Cuban religions such as *santería*, which mix black African beliefs with Catholicism, are said to have a greater hold on Cuban culture. The visit of Pope John Paul II to Cuba in 1998 led to greater tolerance in Cuban society and an increase in the number of practising Roman Catholics. Christmas Day was reinstated as a public holiday in 1997, after 40-odd years of being abolished because it interfered with the sugar harvest.

Because slavery in Cuba was only abolished in 1886, black African traditions were kept alive to a much greater extent than in other Caribbean countries. *Santería* is the most widespread of African faiths (it is also known as Regla de Ocha), and it is based on beliefs such as the existence of spirits that inhabit all plant life. Its origins extend back to the Yoruba slaves from Nigeria who merged their African gods with Catholic saints, so as to be able to worship them without fear of persecution from the Spaniards. Most Catholic saints now have their equivalent African gods. The main *santería* god is Olofi, the creator divinity, who does not have contact with the earth but who is similar to God in christianity. The gods who mediate between him and his followers are called *orishas*, each of whom has his or her own characteristics.

Rituals are performed in people's homes, where altars are set up and decorated with the attributes of the god to whom they are dedicated. For example, the king of *orishas*, the warlike Shangó, will have red flowers, an axe, sword, and bananas at his altar.

Culture

Cultural life in Cuba is one of the most diverse and celebrated of any Latin American country. Cuba has long used its culture as an expression of its national identity. A huge amount of talent exists in the country, developed from its Afro-Caribbean origins and Spanish colonial past, and proudly nurtured since the Revolution.

Sculpture by Mendive in the Museo Nacional de Bellas Artes, Havana

Teatro Roldan, Havana

Music and the arts

The arts, both popular and 'high' art, play an important part in Cuban culture. The government has long recognised the value of nurturing home-grown talent and developing a diverse and vibrant cultural scene. There is a strong Cuban identity in all art forms, especially music, in which Cuba has a very rich heritage. Perhaps one of the biggest achievements is the promotion of the popular arts in daily life.

Ballet

Cuban ballet is highly developed, having its origins in the 1930s. The Ballet Nacional de Cuba performs at the Teatro García Lorca, as well as on the international stage. There is an annual Festival International de Ballet, held in Havana, usually in October.

The main driving force behind Cuban ballet was Alicia Alonso, a ballet dancer and director who established her own ballet company in 1955. Born in 1921, she was famous for her flawless technique and natural expressiveness, performing her most famous roles in the 1940s.

Cinema

Cuban cinema was born in 1959 upon the foundation of the Instituto Cubano del Arte y la Industria Cinematográficos (ICAIC). The ICAIC has been the driving force behind the great success of Cuban cinema since the Revolution. The golden age of Cuban cinema was the 1960s, when the revolutionary government disseminated film culture throughout the country, training film makers and technicians, and showing Cuban films to as wide an audience as

possible. Cuban film directors include Santiago Alvarez, who has made many excellent documentaries, Humberto Solás (who made the classic *Lucía*) and Tomás Gutiérrez Alea. The latter found fame abroad with his famous 1993 film *Fresa y Chocolate* (*Strawberry and Chocolate*), which dealt with issues of dissent and homosexuality. The scarcity of resources available to Cuban film makers has been credited with the high degree of innovation, enthusiasm and non-conformism in Cuban cinema. There are many striking, modern Cuban films, dominated by satire, music and laughter, some of which are shown on long-distance bus journeys. There is an annual ICAIC film festival in Havana,

THE BUENA VISTA SOCIAL CLUB

The film and the music album called *The Buena Vista Social Club* have been credited with the explosion in popularity of Cuban music (and some say of the Cuban tourist industry, too) from 1998 when the musical documentary was released. The film is a nostalgic look at the lives of the band, whose original members are now in their eighties and nineties, and their rehearsals for two international concerts. While much credit must go to the film director Wim Wenders, and to Ry Cooder for bringing the music to an international audience, the stars are the legendary musicians themselves, most now unfortunately deceased; the late Compay Segundo, Ibrahim Ferrer and Rubén González to name just three. Ironically, the album is not for sale in Cuba, due to the nature of the recording contract and label.

An example of 1960s graphic art in the form of a cinema poster

which is now seen as the capital of new Latin American cinema.

Going to the cinema in Cuba is a highly recommended experience as well as being incredibly cheap. The Yara cinema in Vedado, Havana is legendary. 'Must-see' Cuban films include: *Muerte de un Burócrata* (*Death of a Bureaucrat*, Guitiérrez Alea, 1966), a comedy about petty officialdom; *Adorables Mentiras* (*Adorable Lies*, Gerardo Chijona, 1991) a poignant farce about a scriptwriter; *¡Plaff!* (*Splat!*, Juan Cantos Tabio, 1988), a social satire covering many contemporary issues; and of course the Oscar-nominated classic *Fresa y Chocolate* (*Strawberry and Chocolate*, Tomás Gutiérrez Alea, 1993).

Literature

The earliest known work of Cuban literature is *Espejos de Paciencia*, written by Silvestre de Balboa in 1605 about the struggles between a Spanish bishop and a French pirate.

It wasn't until the 19th century that Cuban literature emerged properly with its own identity. José María Heredia (1803–39) was the first of many Cuban writers involved in the struggle for independence from the Spanish, and he is credited with creating Romanticism in the Spanish language. Gertrudis Gómez de Avellaneda (1814–73) wrote the first anti-slavery novel in Latin America: entitled *Sab*, it predated *Uncle Tom's Cabin* by ten years.

The towering figure of 19th-century Cuban literature was José Martí (1853–95), an intellectual, journalist, author and poet. His best known works are *Ismaelillos* and *Versos Sencillos*,

JOSÉ MARTÍ

One of the major icons of anti-colonialism, independence and freedom, José Martí was a poet as well as a freedom fighter. He is best known outside Cuba for the song *Guantanamera*, which utilises Martí's verse. However, his most admired work is *Versos Sencillos* (1891), which developed his style and focused on nature, self-betterment and justice. Born into a poor family in Havana, his fight against colonial injustice was partly as a result of his own suffering; while still a boy, he was sentenced to forced labour for his involvement in an 1868 conspiracy against the Spanish. After a long period of exile which saw him live in Spain, Guatemala, Venezuela and the USA, he returned to Cuba in 1895 at the age of 42. He was welcomed as political leader of the liberation movement but was tragically killed later that year, fighting in the War of Independence.

which express his nationalist ideas in elegant literary form. Many of his prophesies about Cuba's political future have been fulfilled.

The two main Cuban writers in the 20th century were Alejo Carpentier and Nicolás Guillén. Carpentier was one of Cuba's most original authors, and founder of 'Magic Realism', through which he encouraged writers to explore their cultural roots by means of story-telling. His main works include *Los Pasos Perdidos* (*The Lost Steps*), written in 1953, and *The Age of Enlightenment*. Carpentier holds a prominent position among authors in Latin America.

The Museo de Bellas Artes, Havana

Nicolás Guillén was a *mulatto* (of mixed race) poet who exposed the brutal conditions of the black population in the sugar plantations. His work *Motivos de son* (1930) incorporates African rhythms and traditional musical genres such as *son* into his bold, experimental poetry. He was declared National Poet by Fidel Castro, and headed the Union of Cuban Writers.

Other 20th-century literary figures include Virgilio Piñera, a reformer, and José Lezama Lima, a poet and one of the driving forces behind the *criollismo* movement in the 1940s and 1950s, who is best known as author of *Paradiso* (1966).

Among anti-Castro authors in exile, the leading one is Guillermo Cabrera Infante, who wrote *Tres Tristes Tigres*, a witty novel about Havana nightlife during Batista's dictatorship. After the Cuban Revolution, political restrictions were placed on writers, leading to an outcry among intellectuals in Europe. One of the leaders of the more experimental style of literature was Severo Sarduy, whose book *De dónde son los Cantantes* (*From Cuba with a Song*), written in 1967, is regarded as a classic. In recent years, writers have found it easier to express their ideas in public.

Painting

The first stage in the history of Cuban painting began in 1818 with the founding of the San Alejandro Academy of Fine Arts, after which Cuban art began to develop as a separate entity. The second stage in the 1830s was heavily influenced by the European avant-garde, but expressing the new Cuban identity. One of the most famous of Cuban paintings is *Gitana Tropical* (1929) by Victor Manuel, which gave birth to modernism in Cuban art. The island's most famous painter is Wilfredo Lam (1902–82) who dominated the 1940s and who developed his own style using cubism, African masks and surrealism, working for a while with Picasso in Paris.

Other greats during the 1930s and 1940s were Amelia Peláez and René Portocarrero, who were also greatly indebted to the European avant-garde.

In 1959 the National School of Art and the Institute for Advanced Art Studies were founded as part of a government programme of art education. The third stage of Cuban painting has been characterised by the promotion of avant-garde artists, with many talented painters emerging in recent years. International recognition of Cuban art is now growing, helped by art shows like the Havana Biennial. The best place to see colonial and modern art is at the Museo Nacional Palacio de Bellas Artes in Havana.

Shopping for music

For many visitors to Cuba, a whole new world of music listening pleasure is revealed. Music is perhaps Cuba's greatest cultural export, and the following classic albums will either be available in Cuba under the EGREM national label (which has no international distribution rights), or available outside Cuba, under an international label: Afro-Cuban All Stars: *A Toda Cuba le Gusta* and the seminal *Buena Vista Social Club* are both *son* albums with more or less the same line-up of artists playing and are ideal first purchases. Polo Montañez's *Guajiro Natural* is highly popular currently, due to his socially-aware, honest brand of country 'pop' and his tragic death in a car accident in 2002. Salsa fans should look no further than the evergreen Los Van

Van, in particular the 1999 Grammy Award winning *Llego … Van Van* (Van Van is here).

Cuban rap is thriving and the album *Alo Cubano* by Orishas is famed in world-music circles.

A good introduction to Rumba music can be obtained through the compilation by Bis Musica called *La Rumba Soy Yo* – winner of a Grammy Award in 2001.

Other Cuban artists well worth looking out for include Chucho Valdes and his orchestra Irakere (Latin Jazz), Pasio Milanes (Nueva Trova) and Benny Moré, creator of the 'bolero' music style.

Sport

Sports play a significant role in Cuban cultural life. The national sport is baseball, with many Cubans glued to the TV or radio when a big league game is on. Over the years, several Cuban baseball stars have defected to the US, to earn untold riches in comparison to the $200 and less per year that they earn at home. Cuba has one of the best baseball teams in the world and, although amateur, is a match for any professional foreign side.

In other sports, standards are high, due to the government sponsored mass physical education programmes and specialist sporting schools. Cuba is famous on the world stage for athletics, volleyball, basketball and boxing. Sporting legends include Ivan Pedroso, long jump Olympic gold medallist in 2000, Ana Fidelia Quirot, world 800m (2,625ft) champion in the mid 1990s, and Javier Sotomayor, high jump gold medallist at the 1992 Olympics in Barcelona.

Music is an essential part of Cuban culture and everyday life, and few countries have such a rich musical heritage. Everywhere you go, there is music, whether it be salsa from a hi-fi coming from someone's house, or a *son* group playing in the town's *casa de la trova*.

The origins of Cuban music lie in the mixture of European and African cultures which developed in the plantations, villages and ports of the island. African harmony and chorus styles as well as rhythms were absorbed into a vast melting-pot which also included European forms, particularly French and Spanish. The importance of Cuba as a trading centre, particularly in slaves, was behind the fusion of disparate musical elements into new, essentially Cuban genres. The main type of music in Cuba is *son*, which began life in the countryside with the mixing of old songs from Spain and 'call-and-response' choruses from Africa. By the late 1920s, seven-piece bands (*septetos*) were playing *son* with vocal improvisations and a trumpet, and variations were formed, including Guajira son, Bolero son and son Changüí. The most famous example of these is the song 'Guantanamera' in the Guajira style. It is the *septeto* style of *son* that is mostly played in many *casas de la trova* and bars, playing *trova tradicional*, ballad-style songs with guitars.

The first truly Cuban vocal style was the Canción Habanera, which emerged in the 1830s and which produced a number of *canción* styles, including the romantic Bolero. The Nueva Trova style of *canción* reflected the path of the Cuban Revolution, and its principal exponents are Silvio Rodríguez and Pablo Milanés.

Rumba, another highly popular style, originated in poor neighbourhoods as a voice of rebellion against slavery and segregation, and developed in the ports of Havana and Matanzas. It came from a mixture of African rhythm known as

the Yuka, which came from the sugar plantations, and the Spanish Décima. The main urban rumba dances are the stately *yambú* and the more sexual *guaguancó*, while Columbia is more of a country-style dance. Rumba can be a competitive style of music, with rhythms getting faster and faster, with karate moves and break-dancing sometimes finding their way in.

Another strand of Cuban music that emerged was *danzón*, which originated in Matanzas. This was based on European Contradanza with the addition of subtle African rhythms to form a kind of Cuban ragtime. Mambo and Cha cha cha styles emerged directly from *danzón* in the 1940s and 1950s. Different forms of *danzón* are played by contemporary Cuban stars such as Los Van Van and Orquesta Aragón.

Salsa was a development in the 1930s which added the Conjunto style, and the addition of conga drums, timbales, piano and more trumpets, to form more of a 'big band' sound. Salsa is said to combine *son*, rumba and *danzón*, elements of which have been borrowed from jazz and other Latin American genres.

Cuban jazz is one of the most exciting and continually developing music styles, with many young Cuban exiles leading the way in Europe. The King of Cuban Jazz is undoubtedly 'Chucho' Valdés, the virtuoso pianist whose career has spanned more than 30 years. Gonzalo Rubaleaba is another force in Cuban jazz.

The music of the Cuban carnival must be mentioned, being the most vibrant and musical time of the year on the island. The thunderous music of *conga* drives the parade, with both Havana and Santiago having their own styles.

One of the earliest musical forms, the rhythm and songs of Santería is still strong in Cuba. Each deity has their own rhythm, beaten out by African *bata* drums, while songs in the old Yoruba language are still practised and performed.

A more recent development in Cuban music has come to be known as Timba, an urban fusion of different styles including *son*, jazz rock and funk, with lyrical themes about everyday street issues such as prostitution and the struggle to survive. The leading exponent of Timba is NG La Banda, a loose-knit group drawn from long-established bands. The music may sound chaotic, with constantly shifting rhythms, but it provides a challenging alternative to salsa music.

All of these types of music can be heard in Cuba, whether it be at the *casas de la trova*, the *focos culturales*, bars, or in the parks, backyards and on the streets: certainly, the music of Cuba is as vibrant and rich as ever.

Facing page: an ethnic Afro-Cuban performance in Havana

Festivals

There are many festivals, conferences and fiestas in Cuba throughout the whole of the year, and the Buró de Convenciones publishes a five-year list of events with full details. It can be found at *Edificio Focsa, Calle M between 17 & 19, Vedado, Havana* or at *www.buroconv.cubaweb.cu/calendarioe.asp*

Carnival time in Santiago de Cuba

The peak tourist season is from December to the end of March, and July to August. The following will give an idea of the range of festivals available:

January
Liberation Day (national holiday)
Anniversary of the Triumph of the Revolution. *January 1.*

Feria Internacional de Artesanías, Havana
International handicraft fair.

February
Feria Internacional de Libro
Book fair.

March
Festival de Monólogos y Unipersonales, Havana
Monologue acting competition.

Taller Internacional de Teatro de Titeres, Matanzas
Puppeteers' festival.

April
La Huella de España, Havana
Celebration of Spanish-Cuban culture.

Festival de Arte Danzario, Havana and Camagúey
Dance festival.

May
International Workers' Day (national holiday)
May 1.

Primero de Mayo, Havana
May Day rallies and parades.

Fiesta Nacional de la Danza, Santa Clara
Local dance festival.

June
Encuentro de Bandas de Concierto, Bayamo
Outdoor concerts.

Havana Carnival
Parades and music.

Jornada Cucalambeana, Encuentro Festival Iberoamericano de la Décima, Las Tunas.
Cuban rural culture.

July
Festivities in honour of the July 26, 1953 attack on Moncada Garrison (national holiday). *July 25, 26 and 27.*

Fiesta del Fuego, Santiago de Cuba
Culture of Caribbean nations.

Santiago Carnival
Parades and music.

'26 de Julio'
Commemoration of Moncada Barracks attack.

August
Festival Internacional de Música Popular 'Benny Moré', Cienfuegos
Cuban popular music.

September
Hurricane season, Fiesta de la Virgen del Cobre, Santiago de Cuba
Pilgrimage.

Festival de Teatro de La Habana
Theatre performances.

A dancer interpreting the sea deity, Yemayá

October
Beginning of the Wars of Independence (national holiday). *October 10.*

Festival de la Habana de Música Contemporánea
Musical concerts.

Fiesta de la Cultura Iberoamericana, Holguín
Spanish culture.

Festival Internacional de Ballet de La Habana

November
Salón de Arte Cubano Contemporáneo, Havana
Contemporary art.

Festejos de San Cristóbal de La Habana
Commemoration of the founding of the city.

Festival Internacional de Coros, Santiago de Cuba
International choir festival.

December
Christmas Day (national holiday)
December 25.

Festival Internacional del Nuevo Cine Latino-americano, Havana
Film festival.

Fiesta a la Guantanamera, Guantánamo
Afro-Cuban religion.

Parrandas di Remedios, Remedios
Folk festival.

First steps

Many tourists in Cuba stay in their all-inclusive beach resort for most of their trip, which is a shame. Those that make the effort to see the real Cuba will be rewarded with architectural gems, outstanding natural beauty, unspoilt scenery, friendly people, and the intoxicating culture of hip-swaying Cuba rhythms, delicious rum cocktails, vibrant nightlife and a passionate enjoyment of life.

Havana railway station entrance

Culture shock

Visiting Cuba is like entering a different world where even the most seasoned traveller is likely to experience some degree of culture shock. It is best to go with an open mind and a flexible attitude; otherwise you will find Cuba confusing, irrational and full of contradictions! Many of the things that we take for granted in the developed, capitalist world are not to be found in Cuba, or not given a large priority. This is mainly due to the communist nature of the economic and political system, and the long period of economic isolation that the country has endured since the 1960s. However, visitors can easily overcome this initial culture shock and learn a great deal about Cuba and themselves. Cuba challenges our values, our political and economic beliefs, and enables us to appreciate the things that give us comfort in our own world, as well as appreciating the unique culture and society that Cuba has developed over the last 50 years.

The first shock that many visitors encounter happens as soon as they leave the airport upon arrival in Cuba. Many tourists take taxis or coaches from Havana airport at night, driving through the run-down, unlit areas of Havana, passing children and adults socialising or playing in the dusty streets, the doors of their houses ajar, while one glimpses a naked bulb in a living room where the noise from the television or the intoxicating rhythm of salsa music snakes its way into the street. Tourists venturing out into the streets find it hard to understand that they are quite

Tour buses are a great way to see the main sights

safe, even in areas of relative urban decay.

One of the first contradictions that visitors encounter is the fact that Cuban people are generally happy, friendly and fulfilled, despite the apparent lack of material wealth and consumer goods. It is eerie at first to travel around cities where there are no advertising hoardings or posters, or shops of every description tempting us to buy. There is not much of a consumer society in Cuba because the average Cuban does not have the purchasing power to buy much more than the bare essentials to keep their family fed, clothed and housed. Despite this, Cubans have a love of life and a passion for music and socialising that is contagious.

What to do and see

Cuba is a large country and many visitors underestimate its size and the amount that can be done here. Even spending a month on the island will only give you a brief taste of the riches in colonial history, scenery, wildlife and beaches that exist here. Many travellers to Cuba find that only by spending months or years living in the country do they finally start to understand the real Cuba, the one that is unseen and unknown by the tourist. However, there is much to enjoy in Cuba for those that make the effort to venture beyond the all-inclusive package holidays on the island's beach resorts.

Cuba offers a huge range of sights and activities to suit most tastes. There are the historical cities of Havana, Trinidad,

Cuba's provinces and main attractions

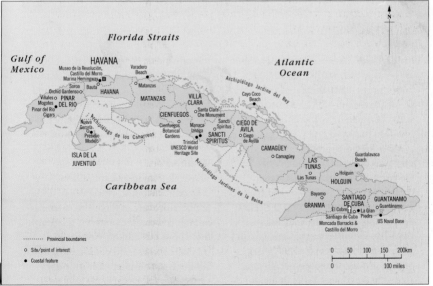

A typical Cuban beach

Santiago de Cuba and Camagüey, there are areas of rich wildlife for nature lovers, particularly the Zapata peninsula, Guanahacabibes and Cayo Coco, and for scuba divers there is María La Gorda, Isla de la Juventud and Cayo Guillermo.

Many foreign visitors come to Cuba on a package holiday based in one of the beach resorts such as Varadero, Guardalavaca or Cayo Coco, and venture to one of the main cities near the resort for a spot of sightseeing and culture. For those staying in Havana or Varadero on a one-week break, a visit to the province of Pinar del Rio to the west of Havana, especially the Viñales Valley, is highly recommended. For a two-week break, you should definitely try to spend at least two days in Trinidad, a colonial treasure and UNESCO World Heritage Site. Also worth visiting, and within striking distance of Havana, are Las Terrazas and Soroa.

When to go

The peak tourist season in Cuba is December to mid-April, when temperatures are at their lowest (warm but not unbearable) and it is relatively dry. The storm and hurricane season begins in August and ends in November, although the number of storms does vary each year. Overall, the climate is relatively mild with lots of warm sunshine. Santiago de Cuba is always a few degrees warmer than the rest of the island, and can be unbearably hot in July and August, although this should not stop you visiting the city for the carnival.

Getting around

Havana and Santiago de Cuba are the main bases from which to see the country, with their good transport links and availability of tours to destinations near and far. Tours offer good value for money: they are a great way to visit attractions out of the city centres, and many hotels have tour desks.

For the more intrepid visitor, travelling long distance by public transport is relatively efficient and cost-effective. While trains are popular, especially between Havana and Santiago

Hiking in the beautiful Viñales Valley

Old American cars are ubiquitous in Havana

de Cuba, long-haul buses are probably the most reliable and comfortable way of travelling between cities. There are internal flights around the country too, which are good value, although delays can occur. It is also possible to hire a car, which has the advantages of greater flexibility, the ability to see more of the country, less cost if there are more than two of you, and the fact that the road traffic is very light. This must be weighed up against the disadvantages of driving in Cuba: poor road signage means that it is easy to get lost, there is a relative scarcity of petrol stations, and you run the risk of breaking down.

How to behave

Cuba has made great strides in the field of tourism over the last decade: there is now a large range of accommodation suitable for all budgets, and getting around the island is fairly easy. While there is not much in the way of tour brochures and promotional material to take away, there are many travel agencies and tour desks that are very helpful. As with everything in Cuba, it is best to be flexible, patient and good-natured about the level of service. There can be a fair amount of bureaucracy and inefficiency, and visitors can be nonplussed by the mechanisms for getting things done. For example, museums may be shut for reasons that no-one can explain, transport may not be available, and things happen with a seemingly invisible hand presiding over them. A smile and a friendly approach will always help, as Cubans are generally very eager to please. As they say in Cuba, '*todo se resuelve*' (everything will resolve itself). Those expecting European or North American levels of service and efficiency will have a frustrating time.

The language

Cubans are a proud people, and for the most part want to create a good impression to foreigners. They will try to speak English where they can, but a few words of Spanish, even if spoken badly, will go a long way in breaking the ice. Learning some Spanish should be the main priority for prospective visitors to Cuba, and the rewards make it worth the effort. Not only does it make it much easier to get around and do things, but it also enables you to get to know Cubans on a more human level and to understand the country better.

Cubans speak Spanish relatively fast in comparison with people in other Latin American countries, with some consonants dropped, especially at the end of words. Young people are more likely to speak good English, and the learning of foreign languages is being encouraged in Cuba, especially for people hoping to work in the tourist sector.

Jineterismo and crime

Compared to most countries in the Americas, Cuba is safe and peaceful. One can walk in the streets at night in Cuban cities, while thefts or other

Accommodation in a *casa particular* such as this is often sought by tourists

crimes against tourists are rare. This is because the punishments are severe for any activity that might harm tourism, and because there is not the level of extreme poverty that is found in other Latin American countries. However, the strong growth in tourism and the fluctuating state of the Cuban economy have made petty crime more common. Bear in mind that the average Cuban will earn about $10–$15 (£6–£9) per month, so any method of obtaining this kind of money in one go is naturally very tempting. It is best to take the same precautions against petty crime in Cuba as one does at home. Never carry large amounts of money with you, leave valuables at your hotel, and keep handbags and day-rucksacks on your front rather than your back, especially in crowded areas.

One phenomenon that has become prevalent in recent years is *jineterismo*. This, in effect, is the practice of living off tourists through the creation of a friendship or relationship. It can range from a man in the street offering anything from cheap cigars, a meal or room for the night, or a *chica* (prostitute), or the *jinetero* or *jinetera* befriending you and offering to help you in any way possible. Many of these 'chance' encounters begin with a question such as 'Where you from, my friend?' One way of recognising a *jinetero* is to judge the effort and speed with which the person tries to establish a friendship, which, at its worst, can feel uncomfortable and pressurising. However, most prospective *jineteros* are harmless and will give up if you are firm but polite, and especially if you can

Main towns and transport links

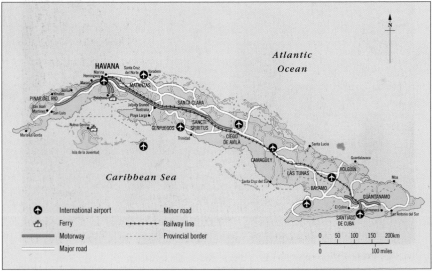

speak some Spanish. The police are cracking down on prostitution and other associations between locals and tourists, and it is common for police officers, in uniform or plain clothes, to operate in tourist areas at night.

Lifestyle

Adapting to the Cuban way of life is one of the pleasures of visiting the country. Cubans enjoy their nightlife, whether it is at a local salsa or *son* venue, walking the streets of the city with friends, or just sitting on the patio at home, enjoying the night-time breeze and watching the activity in the street. Music forms an important part of the Cuban lifestyle, and there is a bewildering array of musical styles, from traditional salsa and *son*, to *charanga* and the more African beats of rumba.

It must be said that Cuba is not noted for its cuisine, due to the economic blockade of the island by the USA and its Latin American partners, which has robbed the island of most of its imported food. Most meals consist of rice with beans, a simple salad, cooked meat (chicken, pork or beef) and either fried plantain or potato. Food cooked in *casas particulares* is typically much better than that in restaurants, and owners will endeavour to buy different types of food in private markets.

Rum is the most popular drink on the island, whether neat, with coke and ice, or other mixes. The *mojito* is a firm favourite and must be tried, if only once. Once you experience a good night out in Cuba with music, dance and rum, you will already feel that you know the island just that bit better.

Take in a cabaret while you're in Cuba!

Havana

Havana is emerging as one of the most colourful and vibrant capital cities in the Caribbean, and is probably the finest example of a Spanish colonial city in the Americas. After decades of neglect, the city was declared a UNESCO World Heritage Site in 1982, and is undergoing a huge facelift, mostly with foreign investment, to restore it to its former architectural glory. It now draws ever-increasing numbers of tourists, attracted by its splendid architecture, bustling nightlife and hugely nostalgic atmosphere.

The José Martí memorial

Before the Revolution in 1959, Havana attracted the megastars of the day to its casinos, glamorous nightlife and hedonistic atmosphere. Since then, time has taken its toll both on the buildings and the economy. There may be no casinos now, but Havana's bars and clubs, with their thriving music scene, are still a major draw for foreigners and Cubans alike.

It must be said that Havana is not a modern city, and visitors expecting fine cuisine and high-class shopping will be disappointed. Many newly-arrived visitors are taken aback by the run-down nature of most of the city, and the poor living conditions of many Cubans. The lack of advertising hoardings or commercial districts is also unsettling at first. On the other hand, the socialist way of life means that the city is unhindered by materialistic pressures, and has a laid-back, contented pace of life.

Havana was founded in 1519, and is situated at the mouth of a deep bay. The city is split into 15 municipalities, of which three contain the main attractions: Habana Vieja (Old Havana) which is the colonial centre, Centro Havana (Central Havana) and Vedado. These three areas are linked by the Malecón, a long road along the seafront.

Dominoes – a popular pastime

PIRATES AND CORSAIRS

From the second half of the 16th century to the end of the 17th, the Spanish had many enemies wishing to share in their newly found wealth in the New World. Pirates were self-employed voyagers who sailed under no nation's flag. Buccaneers such as the Welshman Henry Morgan, the British Sir Francis Drake, and the Frenchman Jacques de Sores, who sacked Havana in 1555, had the permission of their monarch to attack other countries' ships. Corsairs were mercenary ships commissioned and financed by nation states, particularly Britain, France and the Netherlands. These attacks on Spanish galleons and ports led to the building of the impressive fortifications around the main ports, including those in Havana and Santiago de Cuba.

17th-century balcony in Calle Obispo

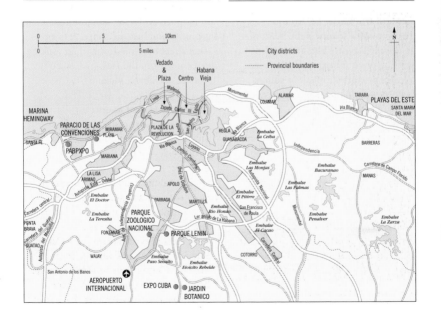

Habana Vieja

The historic heart of Havana was declared part of the 'cultural heritage of humanity' by UNESCO in 1982. After many years of neglect, the former splendour of this district is being restored by the Superintendent of Cultural Heritage, with the aid of foreign investment. This area is characterised by Hispanic-Andalusian architecture, and is in fact the largest colonial centre in Latin America.

Historic architecture

Several days can be spent in Habana Vieja, strolling around the streets or waterfront, and taking in the atmosphere in open-air cafés and restaurants (and being serenaded by visiting musicians). Don't forget to look up at the balconies, which are just as fascinating as life on the ground.

Around the Plaza de Armas

This beautiful square is the heart of the colonial centre and an excellent starting point for exploring Habana Vieja. The elegant, spacious square is lined with Baroque buildings and is full of tropical vegetation. It attracts throngs of visitors and locals alike, who relax on benches or browse around the second-hand book market.

The plaza was built in the 1600s to replace the old Plaza Mayor, the core of Havana's religious, administrative and military life. In the 18th and 19th centuries it became a favourite area for rich Havana citizens to walk around or enjoy carriage rides. The statue in the centre of the square is of Carlos Manuel de Céspedes.

Around the square and in the adjoining streets are some of the most important buildings and sights in the old city, where much careful restoration work has been carried out in recent years.

Calle Obispo

This street is lined with beautiful colonial buildings dating from the 16th to the 19th centuries, including old groceries and historic shops. It is an ideal street to stroll down when walking eastwards from the Havana Centro district to Habana Vieja.

Castillo de la Real Fuerza

This 16th-century castle is the oldest military construction in Havana, and the second oldest fort in the New World. Built to protect the city from pirate attacks, it has a broad moat, angular ramparts and a tower with great views. Inside the castle is a museum with armour and Cuban ceramic art dating from the 1940s onwards (Museo de la Ceramica Cubana). *Plaza de Armas, between O'Reilly and Avenida del Puerto. Tel: 616130. Open: daily 9am–7pm. Small admission charge, free under 12s.*

The Baroque splendour of Palacio de los Capitanes Generales

Museo de la Ciudad
(Palacio de los Capitanes Generales)

On the west side of the Plaza de Armas is the former Palacio de los Capitanes Generales, a superb example of colonial Baroque architecture. The Spanish governors and presidents lived here from its construction in 1780. It now houses the historical museum of the city of Havana, comprising a collection of 19th-century furnishings and memorabilia from the Spanish colonial period. The courtyard contains a statue of Columbus and huge royal palms.

The key sights within the museum include the Cenotaph from the Parroquial Mayor Church, La Giraldilla (the oldest bronze statue in Cuba) and Salón de los Espejos (a 19th-century salon filled with Venetian mirrors).

Calle Tacón 1, west side of Plaza de Armas. Tel: 612876. Open: daily 9am–6pm. Admission charge, separate charges for guided visits and use of cameras/videos, free under 12s.

El Templete

This church is housed in a small neoclassical building built in 1828, and evokes memories of the city's foundations. A column in front of the building commemorates the spot where the first mass was said in 1519 under a ceiba tree, an occasion that is celebrated here every November 16 (*see p49*). All guided tours of La Habana Vieja start here.

Northeast corner of the Plaza de Armas, between Calle Baratillo and O'Reilly. Open: daily 9.30am–6.30pm. Admission charge, free under 12s.

Plaza de la Catedral

Plaza de la Catedral is a beautiful square, with a relaxed atmosphere, where women in colonial costume stroll under the arcades and read fortunes, and with laid-back bars and restaurants where you can listen to live music. The impressive façade of San Cristóbal cathedral is one of the symbols of Old Havana and dominates the square.

In 1592 the first Spanish aqueduct in the New World was built, providing water to local residents and ships docking in the harbour. The cathedral and aristocratic buildings were built in the 18th century.

Bodeguita del Medio

This little bar and restaurant is the most famous in Havana, thanks to the novelist Ernest Hemingway who was a regular here. Meaning 'little shop in the middle', it is exactly halfway along the block. It was in fact founded as a food shop, but soon a bar was added and became a haunt for intellectuals and the stars of the day, including Hemingway, Nat King Cole, and the writer Gabriel García Márquez. It is always busy, and is constantly besieged by tour groups.
Calle Empedrado 207, a few steps away from the cathedral. Tel: 338857. Open: daily 10.30am–midnight.

Habana Vieja

Catedral de San Cristóbal

The Cuban author Alejo Carpentier described the beautiful Baroque façade of this cathedral as 'music turned into stone'. It is certainly grandiose, with two large, asymmetrical bell towers and an abundance of niches and columns. Construction of the cathedral began in 1748 under the Jesuits, but it only received its current name in 1796 when, according to popular belief, the relics of

Christopher Columbus were housed here until 1898. In comparison to the façade, the neoclassical interior is disappointing. *Calle Empedrado 156. Tel: 617771. Open Mon–Tue, Thur–Sat 9.30am–12.30pm, Sun 8.30am–12.30pm, mass at 10.30am.*

Museo de Arte Colonial
This 18th-century colonial mansion houses a fascinating museum of Colonial art, and contains furniture, chandeliers, porcelain and other items from various 18th- and 19th-century aristocratic houses in Havana, combining European, Creole and colonial traditions. It also includes an exquisite collection of stained-glass windows (*mediopunto*).
Calle San Ignacio 61. Tel: 626440. Open: daily 9am–6.45pm. Admission charge, free under 12s.

El Floridita bar and restaurant, opposite Parque Central – once a haunt of Hemingway

Plaza de San Francisco

With a little imagination, from this square you can view the port in days gone by, full of galleons loaded with gold and other cargo, about to set sail for Spain. The original commercial nature of this Andalusian-style square can be seen in two buildings, the old customs house (Aduana General de la Republica) and the former stock exchange (Lonja del Comercio).

Basilica Menor de San Francisco de Asis

The most important building in the square is this massive military-looking building, built in the 16th century but partly rebuilt in the 1700s. The bell tower (*campanario*) has marvellous views of the city and the port, and was at the time a landmark for returning voyagers and a lookout for pirates. The building is now used as a concert hall for choral and chamber music. The convent is now a museum of holy art, and has recently been restored.

Calle Oficios. Tel: 629683. Museum open daily 9am–6.30pm. Admission charge for museum, bell tower and for taking photos/video. Tickets for concerts are available here, free under 12s.

Fuente de los Leones

Set in the middle of the square, this fountain is modelled on one found in the Alhambra, in Granada, Spain. It was donated to the city in 1836, and

The stunningly restored Plaza Vieja

for many years it supplied the ships docked here with drinking water.

Other sights in Habana Vieja
Convento de Santa Clara

One of the oldest and most typical of colonial religious buildings in the New World, the convent covers four blocks of Habana Vieja. The plain exterior belies a more extravagant interior, with carefully preserved cloisters, nuns' cells and patios overflowing with vegetation.

It was founded in 1644 by nuns from Cartagena in Colombia, and offered refuge to the poorer girls of the city. For a time, between 1919 and 1982, the building housed the Ministry of Public Works, but it was then decided to return the building to its former glory, a project which still continues today.
Calle Cuba 610, between Calles Sol and Luz. Tel: 615043. Open: Mon–Fri 8.30am–5pm. Admission charge, free under 12s.

Feria del Tacón

An interesting and colourful stroll can be had around this, the largest craft market in the city, even if you don't buy anything. The list of products available, from souvenirs to carvings and jewellery, is endless, and you may find yourself spending longer here than you anticipated! It does get very warm here, so remember to bring drinks to cool you down.
Avenida Tacón, between Chacon and Empedrado, at the end of Plaza de la Catedral. Open: Wed–Sat 10am–6pm.

Fundación Destilería Havana Club

Visitors can see the production process in this distillery of the most famous

---

THE BEST VIEWS OF HAVANA

1 Looking from the top-floor swimming pool of the Hotel NH Parque Central towards the Capitol building in the morning light.
2 From José Martí Memorial, Plaza de la Revolución, looking over Old Havana.
3 Sitting in the garden terrace at the Hotel Nacional, looking down on the Malecon in the softening rays of the late-afternoon sun.
4 Looking westwards towards Havana from Castillo del Morro, best seen in the morning.
5 From the Hotel Havana Libre top-floor restaurant in the afternoon or early evening, with breathtaking views over the whole city.

---

brand of Cuban rum. The fermentation, distillation, filtering and ageing processes are all covered in the tour, with the chance to taste samples of what one Cuban writer described as 'the cheerful child of sugar cane'.
Calle San Pedro 262, between Sol and Murralla. Tel: 618051. Open: Mon–Thur 9am–5pm, Fri–Sun 9am–4pm. Admission charge, free under 16s.

Plaza Vieja

This square is dazzling in its restored Spanish colonial beauty. It was originally laid out in 1559 and known as 'New Square', and it was the city's main public square until the 19th century. It has many fine buildings with elegant balconies overlooking the fountain in the middle. The best balcony from which to admire the view is La Casona (house of the former Conde de Ricla).

Walks: Habana Vieja

Habana Vieja has so many beautiful streets and buildings of interest that you can wander the streets aimlessly and bump into them at virtually every turn. However, to help recognise those of most interest and give some background detail, here are two walks that can either be taken consecutively or on separate days. They would easily fill a whole day, although a break is advised for a well-earned lunch break!

Walk 1: Around Plaza de Armas and Plaza de la Catedral (*see green route on page 50*)
Allow 3 hours minimum.
Begin at La Maqueta de la Habana Vieja, in Mercaderes (between Obispo and Obrapia), very near the Plaza de Armas.

1 La Maqueta de la Habana Vieja
This scale model of the city (built in the proportions of 1:500) offers an overview of the area. There are light and sound effects to replicate a day in the city.
Walk northwards on Mercaderes and turn right onto Obispo, which leads onto the Plaza de Armas. On your left is the Palacio.

2 Palacio de los Capitanes Generales
Now the Museo de la Ciudad (City Museum), this fine Baroque palace houses one of the key museums in Havana, offering an overview of the city's history. In front of this palace, there are often displays of dance or other activities to interest tourists and locals alike, organised by the city council.
With the square in front of you, turn left to the end of the block, left again onto O'Reilly and first right onto Mercaderes. At the T-junction, turn left into Plaza de la Catedral.

3 Catedral de San Cristóbal
The Baroque façade of this church, declared a national monument, is considered one of the most beautiful in Latin America. On either side are two bell towers (the west one is half as wide as the east one), which provide fine views.
Turn right out of the Cathedral and walk towards Calle Empedrado.

4 Bodeguito del Medio
Although only small, this bar simply oozes character, and is popular with tour groups. It was a regular haunt of Ernest Hemingway, whose favourite tipple here was the *mojito* (*see p53*).
Turning back to the Plaza de la Catedral, walk to the south of the square.

5 Museo de Arte Colonial
It would be hard to find a better example of early colonial domestic architecture than this building. Dating from 1720, it houses an exhibition of colonial furniture and objects.
Turning left out of the museum, turn onto San Ignacio and walk southwards, turning left onto O'Reilly, and walk on the left-hand side of the Plaza de Armas. Follow it round as it turns left.

6 Castillo de la Real Fuerza

First built in 1558, this is the oldest building in Cuba. It is worth walking around its characteristic angular ramparts, and climbing the tower to enjoy fine views of the city.

Coming out from the castle, cross the road and you will see a narrow street between the buildings. Walk down this street, Calle Enna, the narrowest and shortest street in the city, named after a general from colonial times. Keep the Plaza de Armas on your right.

7 El Templete

Another important building in Havana's history, this austere building stands on the spot where, according to legend, the city of San Cristóbal de la Habana was founded in 1599. It was also here, under a ceiba tree (*see p43*), that the first meeting of the local government was held.

If you feel you deserve a spot of luxury, the Hotel Santa Isabel is the perfect place to enjoy good views of the Plaza de Armas with lunch or a cocktail.

Façade of the Catedral de San Cristóbal

Walks around Habana Vieja

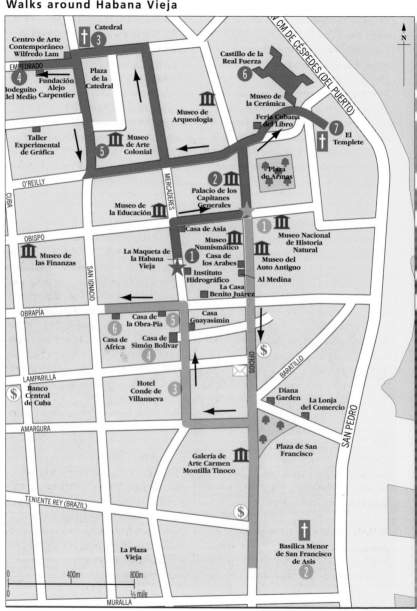

Walk 2: Around Plaza de San Francisco (*see orange route opposite*)
Allow up to 2 hours.
The tour starts in Plaza de Armas, on the south side, where Calle Oficios begins.

1 Calle Oficios

This is one of the most atmospheric streets in Havana, and recipient of much needed restoration work to its buildings. It was originally a link between the military centre of Plaza de Armas and Plaza de San Francisco, the commercial port area. There are many buildings of interest, including the Museo Numismático (coins) at No 8, the Casa de los Arabes (ethnographic Hispanic-Arabic objects) at No 16, and Museo del Auto Antiguo (vintage cars).
Continuing south will bring you to Plaza de San Francisco.

2 Basilica Menor de San Francisco de Asis

The Basilica Menor de San Francisco de Asis is the most important building in this square. Built in the 16th century, it started life as home to the Franciscan community, but is now a concert hall on account of its exceptional acoustics. There are great views from the bell tower.
Back at the northwest corner of the square, take Amargura going west, and turn right onto Mercaderes.

3 Hotel Conde de Villanueva

The quiet courtyard of this charming hotel is an ideal place for a quick break from the bustle and heat of the Havana streets. It was once the residence of the Count of Villanueva in the 18th century, who promoted tobacco abroad and helped to bring the railway to Cuba. The hotel includes a cigar shop as well as a good restaurant.
Continue north on Mercaderes, crossing Lamparilla, and look to the left of the street.

4 Casa de Simon Bolivar

Simon Bolivar is a key figure in South American history, a protestor against Spanish rule, and former resident of this house. There are exhibits about his life, and also some Venezuelan art.
Continue north on Mercaderes and turn left onto Obrapía.

5 Casa de la Obra-Pía

The house name means 'charity', after the altruistic actions of a wealthy Spanish nobleman in the 17th century, who gave a generous dowry to five orphan girls every year, so that they could either get married or enter a convent. This yellow building is regarded as one of the finest examples of Cuban Baroque architecture. The house displays furniture from the 18th and 19th centuries, and was originally built in 1665.
A few yards away on the same street, at No 157, is the Casa de Africa.

6 Casa de Africa

This 17th-century building exhibits many objects from the various ethnic groups that were shipped to Cuba as slaves. It includes paintings of plantation life, objects from Afro-Cuban cults, and instruments of torture. It is ironic that the building used to be the residence of a family of plantation owners on the upper floor, and a tobacco factory worked by slaves on the ground floor.

Cuban rum

The origins of Cuban rum date back to the 1500s when alcohol was produced from sugar-cane juice. Sugar had been introduced to Cuba by Christopher Columbus, who brought sugar-cane roots from the Canary Islands.

In the 19th century, a new distillation process was introduced which considerably improved the quality of the drink, and Cuba became internationally famous for its rum. The most famous rum family was the Bacardí family, who dominated the rum industry in Cuba for nearly 100 years.

The process of rum-making begins with the dilution of molasses, the sticky amber paste which is a by-product of sugar. The diluted mixture is fermented with yeasts, then distilled and filtered to produce an *eau de vie*. After 18 months, purified water and pure alcohol are added, producing a young, clear rum known as 'Silver Dry', which is generally used in cocktails.

Other types of rum include Carta Blanca (aged for three years), Carta Oro (five years) and Añejo (seven years). Older rum is usually drunk neat or on the rocks, and is of better quality than young rum.

Cocktails became popular after 1870 when ice-making was developed in the USA, and the 'Cuba Libre' was invented when American soldiers brought bottled cola drinks to Cuba at the end of the 19th century. The *daiquirí* cocktail was invented by an engineer in the Daiquirí mines in eastern Cuba, and cocktails were especially popular in the 1920s with the influx into Cuba of people from all over the world, especially Americans escaping prohibition.

Rum is an integral part of Cuban life, and it is enjoyed at parties and festivities, as well as being offered to the gods of *santería*. An ideal place to learn more about Cuban rum is at the distilleries of Havana Club, the most famous brand of Cuban rum. Tours begin in the courtyard of the Havana Club Foundation, in Habana Vieja.

The most famous cocktail in Cuba, which is particularly delicious in the warm climate, is the refreshing *mojito*. No two *mojitos* will taste the same, although the place to be seen drinking one is at the Bodeguita del Medio i Havana, made famous by Ernest Hemingway.

To make a *mojito*, take a tall glass, mix together half a tablespoon of sugar, the juice of half a lime, and lightly crushed mint leaves. Add 1.5oz (43g) of light dry rum, ice cubes and top up with soda water. Garnish it with a mint leaf and serve with a straw. Other rum cocktails that tourists will come across include: the Havana Especial (pineapple juice, maraschino liqueur and light dry rum), Mulata (lime juice, crème de cacao, extra aged rum), Ernest Hemingway Special (lime, grapefruit juice, maraschino liqueur, light dry rum, and served like a Daiquirí).

Facing page: rum is the basis for cocktails such as *mojitos*

Centro Havana

The boundary between Old Havana and Central Havana (Centro) is blurred, with Parque Central and the Capitolio lying on this border. There is certainly a change of atmosphere from Habana Vieja, and the area is less quaint, more spacious and less obviously aimed at tourists.

The Capitolio

Parque Central
Parque Central itself is used as a popular meeting place for locals to discuss sport (mainly baseball), music and politics. Here the locals may try to befriend you by suggesting a *mojito* at a nearby bar, for which they would receive a commission from the bar.

Capitolio
One of the most imposing buildings in Latin America, the Capitolio dominates the Havana skyline, and is worth a visit in order to wander around the grandiose interior. It was built in 1929 by the dictator Machado in the style of the US Capitol building in Washington DC and was the seat of parliament until 1959.
Paseo de Martí (Prado). The only entrance is from the steps on the east side. Tel: 603411. Open: daily 8am–8pm, although it often shuts early. Admission charge, tours available. Free under 12s.

Gran Teatro de la Habana
With a magnificent façade, this is one of the world's largest opera houses. It was designed by Belgian architect Paul Belau to host the social activities of the city's wealthy Spanish community at the time. Part of the Palacio del Centro Gallego from 1915, it continues in its role as a concert hall and theatre.
Paseo de Martí (Prado). Tel: 613077. Open: Tue–Sun 9.30am–5pm. Admission charge.

Hotel Inglaterra
This lovingly restored historic hotel is a national monument. Although the architecture is 19th-century neoclassical, it has Moorish elements, with beautiful Seville tiles inside.
Paseo de Martí (Prado) 416, on the corner of San Rafael. Tel: 608595.

Paseo de Martí (Prado)
This picturesque boulevard is similar to Las Ramblas in Barcelona, and it is ideal for a gentle stroll in the shade of the trees. Laid out in 1772 outside the city walls, it soon became popular with city aristocrats who took carriage rides here.
Paseo de Martí (Prado) runs north from Parque Central to the Castilla de la Punta by the sea.

Other sights in Central Havana
Museo Nacional de Bellas Artes
This is perhaps the finest museum in Cuba with almost 50,000 works of art

from all over the world. The building underwent a five-year refurbishment and re-opened in 2001, dividing its collections between the original palacio and the Palacio del Centro Asturiano, two blocks away by the Parque Central. Highlights of the museum include works by Gainsborough, Velazquez, Murillo and Hans Memling.

Palacio (original building) on Trocadero, between Zuleta and Avenida de las Misiones. Features Cuban Art. Tel: 613858. Open: Tue–Sat 10am–6pm, Sun 10am–2pm. Admission charge, free under 12s. Centro Asturiano on San Rafael, between Zuleta and Avenida de las Misiones. Features World Art. Admission details as above.

Museo de la Revolución

It is surely no coincidence that the museum recounting the history of the Cuban Revolution is housed in the former presidential palace of the US-backed dictator Batista. The museum shows the fascinating story of Cuban political development, from the slave uprisings to the period of cooperation with the former Soviet Union. The grounds house the yacht *Granma*, which carried Castro and his companions to launch the revolution in 1956.

Calle Refugio, between Monserrate and Zuleta. Tel: 613858. Open: daily 10am–5pm. Admission fee and charges for a recommended guided tour (as displays are mostly in Spanish), free under 12s.

Walk: Centro Havana

While the romantic little streets of Habana Vieja mostly hark back nostalgically to the colonial days of the 19th century, Centro relates mostly to the first half of the 20th century. It has a different atmosphere which is more gritty and in a sense more reflective of life in Cuba's capital city. *Allow 3 hours for the walk, although it can be extended to include a walk down the Malecón, the city's seafront.*

1 Capitolio
The Capitol building is a symbol of the city, dominating the area with its neoclassical elegance. The home of the government since its opening in 1932 until 1959, the sumptuous interior is well worth visiting, and is an ideal spot for a drink in the café, which has a grandstand view of the bustle of everyday life in Paseo de Martí below.
At the bottom of the steps, turn left and walk up Paseo de Martí (Prado) towards the grand building in front of you.

2 Gran Teatro de la Habana
Once host to the social activities of the city's wealthy Spanish community, this building continues its role as concert hall and theatre. The impressive façade includes four sculpture groups depicting Charity, Education, Music and Theatre.
Continue walking north, past Calle San Rafael on your left.

3 Hotel Inglaterra
Despite the British name, this 19th-century hotel is definitely inspired by Spain. While admiring the regal

interior, it is tempting to soak up the atmosphere in one of its four cafés and restaurants.
From the hotel, cross the road to the leafy park opposite.

4 Parque Central
This pleasant park is surrounded by grand hotels and historical buildings, and is a gathering place for locals to relax under the shady trees and let an hour or two pass discussing important matters (mostly sport!). The statue in the centre is of Jose Martí, one of Cuba's national heroes.
Facing north, you can see the long boulevard of Paseo de Martí.

5 Paseo de Martí (Prado)
An ideal place to stroll down at any time of day, and especially popular with locals at sunset, this lovely boulevard continues all the way up to the Malecón on the seafront. There are many attractive buildings, including a neo-Moorish building on the left-hand side, on the corner of Calle Virtudes.
Continue walking north, and look right after passing Calle Empedrado.

6 Hotel Sevilla

This Moorish building is a historic hotel which first opened in 1908. The bar on the top floor is a great spot from which to enjoy the views over the Malecón.

Continue to the end of the Paseo de Martí (Prado) towards the Castilla de la Punta, where the Malecón begins and turn left.

7 Malecón

This seafront promenade represents Havana more than any other place. It is also a gathering point for locals. Some of the buildings along it are being restored, while others are losing the battle against the destructive sea air. The Malecón continues for 7km (just over 4 miles) from the colonial centre through Centro and into Vedado.

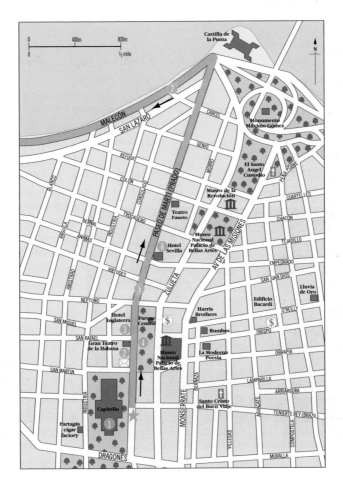

In the 16th century a network of fortresses was established around the coast of Cuba to protect Spanish possessions from pirate attacks. Tourists can visit many of these fortresses, including the Castillo de la Real Fuerza in Havana.

The oldest house in Cuba, Diego de Velázquez's residence in Santiago de Cuba, was built in 1522. Simple wooden dwellings built before this time were gradually replaced by stone-built *mudéjar*-style houses. By the 17th century, many private homes had thick walls, tiled roofs and shuttered windows, all of which gave protection from the tropical sun and heavy rain. Central courtyards and wooden balconies reflected Spanish influence.

The 18th century is seen as the golden age of Cuban architecture, characterised by the Baroque style imported from Europe. The most notable Baroque building in Havana is the Cathedral, built in 1777, and many churches were built during the 17th and 18th centuries, reflecting the great power of the church at that time. Highlights of civic Baroque architecture in Havana include the Palacio de los Capitanes Generales and the Palacio del Segundo Cabo. The *mediopunto* style of stained-glass windows was developed in the mid 18th century to protect houses from the tropical sun.

Neoclassical architecture was predominant in the 19th century, characterised by porticoes with columns and lintels, wrought iron and decoration inspired by classical antiquity and the Renaissance. The first neoclassical building in Havana was the Templete, a

small doric temple in the Plaza de Armas. Other good examples of this style are the Palacio de Aldama in Havana and the Teatro Santo in Matanzas.

Between the 19th and 20th centuries, there was a mix of architectural styles, in both public and private buildings. The most notable of these are the Capitolio in

Havana, the neo-Moorish Palacio de Valle in Cienfuegos and the splendid Havana mansions at Paseo and Calle 17, including the Casa de la Amistad.

Art Nouveau and Art Deco architecture were popular in the early 20th century, the best example being the sumptuous Edificio Bacardí in Habana Vieja, while other examples are on the Malecón in Santiago de Cuba.

The most popular architect in the 1950s was Aquiles Capablanca, who was inspired by le Corbusier, and his Tribunal de Cuentas in Havana is one of the most admired 20th-century buildings in Latin America. Another stunning building is the Tropicana nightclub in Miramar, built in 1952 by Max Borges Jr. Tall skyscrapers were also built around this time, including the Habana Libre and Riviera hotels.

The Revolution saw the conversion of old private buildings for public use rather than the construction of new buildings, for example, the Moncada Garrison in Santiago which is now a school and museum. The influence of Soviet architecture can also be seen, with adaptations to the buildings to take account of the Cuban climate. Many state-run hotels were built in the 1960s and 1970s.

A good overview of the development of Havana's architecture can be obtained by viewing the scale model of the city, which is situated at La Maqueta de la Habana, Calle 28 113, between Calles 1 and 3.

Facing page: the Baroque Cathedral, Havana
This page: 19th-century neoclassical Palacio de Aldama, Havana

Vedado and Plaza

The areas of Vedado and Plaza (the area around Plaza de la Revolución) fulfil many roles. Firstly, they represent the city's political and cultural centre, containing Plaza de la Revolución, the venue for major celebrations and political gatherings. They also contain many buildings of interest, from early 20th-century mansions to large hotels made famous in the 1950s through their glamour and their links with the mafia. Vedado is the place to be for the best nightlife and cultural events.

Cover of a children's periodical by José Martí

The name Vedado means 'prohibited' in Spanish, a reference to its 16th-century origins, when it was forbidden to build houses in the area, so that a full view of approaching pirates or invaders could be had. Vedado expanded extensively from the late 19th century, when many of the city's leading families set up residence in the area.

Vedado sights
Memorial Jose Martí

While the monument itself is not to everyone's taste, the views from the top – the monument is over 100m (328ft) tall – and the impressive museum at the base make this an unmissable sight in modern Havana. Work on the monument began in 1953, on the 100th anniversary of the birth of Cuba's national hero. The memorial at the base contains memorabilia and portraits of Martí, while the lobby features some of the patriot's thoughts.
Plaza de la Revolución. Tel: 592351. Open: Mon–Sat 9am–5pm. Admission charge, free under 12s.

Museo de Artes Decorativas

This impressive museum is worth visiting for its French Rococo and Louis XV furnishings, its lovely inner gardens, and the Regency-inspired dining room, complete with a grand dinner service owned by dictator Batista. This was the former residence of the Countess de Revilla de Camargo, one of the wealthiest Cuban women in the 20th century, who collected fine art and held elegant society dinners. It houses some beautiful art from Europe and the Far East, including a desk that once belonged to Marie Antoinette. The pink marble Art Deco bathroom is wonderful!
No 502, Calle 17, corner of Calle E. Tel: 308037. Open: Tue–Sat 11am–6pm, Sun 9.30am–1pm. Admission charge, free under 12s.

Necrópolis Colón

One of the largest cemeteries in the world, the Necrópolis Colón houses a wealth of funerary art and is a national monument. Also known as Cementerio Colón (Columbus Cemetery), it

contains 2 million graves, equal to the city's current population. Dating from 1886, it was designed by Spanish architect Calixto de Loira and the main entrance features a statue in Carrara marble of the three virtues, Faith, Hope and Charity, sculpted in 1904.
Entrance is on Zapata and Calle 12. Tel: 321050. Open: daily 8am–5pm. Admission charge.

Plaza de la Revolución
This massive square is not one of the most beautiful, but is worth visiting for its importance, both historically and politically. It was originally designed in 1952 and most of the buildings around it are from this time.

It is here that the major rallies and speeches for Havana are held, and the square can hold around 1 million people. The first rally was held in January 1959 following victory in the Cuban Revolution, and Pope John Paul II celebrated mass here in January 1998.

Every year on the morning of May 1, Fidel Castro addresses a million people to celebrate International Labour Day.

The national monument of Necrópolis Colón

Walk: Vedado district, Havana

Vedado is a busy, largely residential area of broad avenues, with a real mix of architectural styles, from ugly 1950s high-rises to crumbling neoclassical mansions. The area houses many government offices as well as the university, which makes it a lively part of town, especially at night. The main avenue here is Calle 23, known as La Rampa, modern Havana's best-known street.

Allow 2¹/₂ hours.

The walk starts at Hotel Nacional. This walk does not include any museums, but nevertheless provides an insight into the many different sides of modern Havana. The walk is ideal in the afternoon, when the views of Habana Vieja are at their best.

1 Hotel Nacional

Perhaps the most elegant and famous of Havana's hotels, this building has retained most of its 1930s atmosphere, when the great and the good stayed here. The bar on the ground floor has photographs of its famous guests, including some Mafia legends who financed the building of the hotel in 1930. The terrace at the bottom of the superb gardens has a beautiful view of virtually the whole length of the Malecón.

Walk along Calle 23 (known as La Rampa) westwards until you reach Calle N.

2 Hotel Habana Libre

The Habana Libre is one of the biggest and most visible of the city's hotels. It was inaugurated in 1958 as the most modern and decadent hotel in the capital, but was taken over by Fidel Castro when the Revolution came to Havana in January 1959, and used for a short while as his headquarters. There are some fascinating historical photos in the lobby.

Continue walking up La Rampa until you reach a park on your right with queues of people at all times of the day.

3 Coppelia ice cream

Queuing at this famous ice cream parlour is a long-established social ritual for local residents. This large glass and metal building was the famous location in one of Cuba's most well-known films *Fresa y Chocolate* (*Strawberry and Chocolate*).

Continue walking westwards on La Rampa for a couple of blocks, and look out for a park on your left.

4 Parque del Quijote

The main feature in this tree-filled area is the statue of Don Quixote. This nude figure on horseback was designed by Sergio Martinez.

Carry on walking along La Rampa and turn right when you reach Calle G (Avenida de los Presidentes). This wide avenue takes you down to the Malecón where you turn left, walking two blocks.

5 Feria de Malecón

This busy market is full of handicrafts, souvenirs and books, and well worth wandering around. It is open until 6.30pm daily except Wednesdays. Don't be tempted to take up the offers of illegal cigar sellers that operate here.
Continue walking along the Malecón for a few blocks until you reach Calle Paseo on your left. Walk up this elegant avenue until you reach Calle 15. Turn right and walk three blocks.

6 Parque John Lennon

The main feature in this peaceful park is a bronze statue of John Lennon, sitting on a bench, with words from *Imagine* etched on the ground. Sculpted by José Villa, it was inaugurated in December 2000 by Fidel Castro. The park is sometimes used as a venue for classical guitar concerts.
Walk back towards Calle Paseo on Calle 17 (going eastwards). Once on Calle Paseo, look right.

7 Casa de la Amistad

Ideal for a drink, dinner and dancing, this cultural centre is housed in a sumptuous Art Deco building. Originally owned by Pedro Baro, it was given to his mistress Caterina Lasa in the early 1900s.

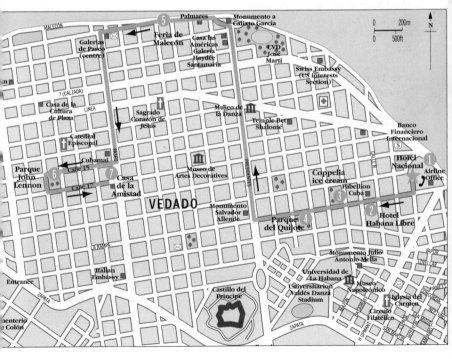

Havana environs and excursions

There are many interesting places to visit just a taxi ride from the city centre, or as part of an organised tour booked through hotel tourist desks. These give a different picture to the one experienced in Havana alone, and are a good way of taking a break from the city.

Hotel Nacional, Havana

Castillo de Morro viewed from the Malecón

HAVANA ENVIRONS
Castillo de Morro

This is one of the most visible landmarks in Havana, especially from the Malecón, with one of the best views back towards the city. It stands on the headland to the northeast of the city in the district of Casablanca. It was constructed in the 17th century and was one of the main fortifications built by the Spanish to protect the natural harbour from pirates and foreign invaders. It is now a museum exhibiting Cuban history since the arrival of Columbus.

Within the grounds is the Battery of the 12 Apostles. There is a display of Afro-Cuban dancing and music every Saturday between 10 and 11pm.
You can take a taxi from the city, or take any bus going through the tunnel from San Lazaro and Avenido del Puerto. Get off at the stop after the tunnel, cross the road and climb to the left following the path. Open: daily 8.30am–8.30pm (Museum 10am–6pm). Separate admission charges for the park, castle, lighthouse, and for photos/video.

Cojímar

The main reason for visiting this former seaside village is to retrace the footsteps of Ernest Hemingway, who used it as the setting for his great novel *The Old Man and the Sea*, and who was a regular in the streets and bars. The village has lost some of its charm, although there are some points of interest. There is a bust of Hemingway in a small square that bears his name, a faithful copy of the one in El Floridita bar in Havana. The bust was paid for with donations from

his fishermen friends. Hemingway's favourite restaurant, La Terraza, can still be visited. It is still worth a drink here, if only for a look at the photographs that cover the wall, and to sample the elegant atmosphere.

On the seafront, there is a small 17th-century fort, designed by Giovanni Battista Antonelli, the architect of the Castillo de Morro.
Cojímar is a 15-minute taxi ride from Havana.

Fortaleza de San Carlos de la Cabana

A short walk from Castillo de Morro, this fortress is worth a visit if only to experience the cannon-firing ceremony (nightly at 9pm), recalling the closure of the city walls to protect it from attack. With a vertical wall of 700m (2,300ft), this famous fortress dominates the entrance to the city harbour. It was built in 1774 and was at the time the largest the Spanish had built in the Americas. In its heyday, 120 cannon were positioned within the fortress walls.

There are two museums, the first about the fortress, and the second about Che Guevara, who triumphantly took possession of the fortress in 1959 at the end of the Cuban Revolution.
The fortress is within walking distance of the Castillo de Morro or via the district of Casablanca. Open: daily 10am–10pm. Admission charge.

Miramar

Located 16km (10 miles) west of the old city, Miramar is the most elegant part of Havana, as it was before the Revolution, when the city's richest inhabitants lived here. The southern part is also home to the internationally famous 'Tropicana' cabaret show, as well as excellent restaurants and music venues.

Most of the embassies and consulates are here, with lots of offices, especially for multinational joint ventures, while modern developments are springing up, catering mostly for business people. It is understandably the most desirable residential area in the city. Life in this quarter revolves around the busy Avenida 5, a broad, tree-lined avenue flanked by splendid early 20th-century villas and newer hotels.

Miramar is easily accessed by private car, taxi or bus.

Playas del Este

This is the name for the string of beaches outside Havana – one of the few cities in the world to have sizeable beaches only a 20-minute drive from the city centre. They consist of 50km (31 miles) of fine sand and clear water, offering good tourist facilities. They are a good compromise for people who want to spend some of their time at the seaside during their visit to Havana, but who don't want to travel too far. The best – and most popular – beach is Santa María del Mar, which is lined with pine and coconut trees and has very good facilities for water sports, plus a good selection of hotels.

Guanabo is a more traditional beach with small houses, restaurants and shops. At weekends, this is the liveliest place along the coast, when *Habaneros* (residents of Havana) congregate here. *The Playas del Este can be accessed by hiring a private car for the day if there are two or more people; otherwise, tours can be booked at relatively low cost through tourist offices.*

Santa María del Mar, Playas del Este

Finca la Vigía – Hemingway's library

San Francisco de Paula (Finca la Vigía)

Hemingway fans should visit the writer's only residence outside the USA, situated on the outskirts of Havana. The villa has been surprisingly well preserved, and contains virtually all the original objects and decorations. The villa was turned into a public museum in 1962, upon the news of Hemingway's suicide in the USA.

There is a library with 8,000 books, hunting trophies, artworks, and even the author's pipe and typewriter. The fact that these objects have been left as they were creates a lived-in, homely atmosphere. Two curious features of the house include a cat cemetery in the garden (the author had 60 cats during his lifetime) and Hemingway's fishing boat, the *Pilar*, scene of many a drunken fishing trip.

Finca la Vigía is 11km (6¹/₂ miles) from the centre of Havana. It can be visited by taxi or by taking Bus P1 from Linea and P2 from the corner of 26 and 41 streets in Vedado. Tel: 910809. Open: daily except Tue and Sun 9am–4pm. Admission charge to view the interiors through open windows and doors. (There are no toilets.)

Walk: Miramar quarter, Havana

Miramar is an ideal place for a relaxing stroll where you can take in the broad avenues and elegant buildings of this relatively wealthy suburb. It also gives a contrasting impression to the more compact, run-down streets of Havana.

Allow 3 hours.

Begin from the fort, Fuerte de Santa Dorotea de la Luna en la Chorrera, a national monument in the Vedado district, on the east side of the River Almendares. You may wish to take a break halfway through the walk for lunch or a snack – there are several good places to eat.

1 Fuerte de Santa Dorotea de la Luna en la Chorrera
This fort was crucial to the city's defence system for more than two centuries, and was built in 1645 by Giovanni Battista Antonelli, the famous Spanish military engineer.
Opposite the fort is the next landmark.

2 The 1830 restaurant
The building for this restaurant was once the home of Carlos Miguel de Céspedes, the Minister of Public Works under President Machado, one of the US-backed dictators before the Revolution. The restaurant is recommended.
Walk down to Calle 11 and over the iron bridge to reach the Miramar area. Turn right and go up to Avenida 5 (Quinta Avenida).

3 Avenida 5
This broad, tranquil boulevard with shrubs and benches is flanked on both sides by large, imposing mansions built in the early 20th century. During the Revolution, these private houses were abandoned by the escaping upper classes or seized by the government who turned them into public buildings.
Walk up the Avenida, to the corner of Calle 26.

4 Iglesia de Santa Rita
There are three distinctive tall arches in the façade of this modern church, while to the left of the entrance is a statue of St Rita by Cuban sculptress Rita Longa.
Walk up to Calle 28 and turn right, then turn left on Avenida 3 (Tercera). On the right is an interesting museum.

5 Maqueta de la Habana
A great way to get an overview of the city, this scale model of Havana was opened in 1995 and is now a great attraction. The development of Havana from colonial times onwards is shown here, with different colours representing construction periods.

Continue to walk westwards along Avenida 3, then turn right to walk one block up to Avenida 1 (which runs parallel), which is the seafront. Walk along Avenida 1 until you reach the corner of Calle 60, on your left.

6 Acuario Nacional

The city aquarium is housed in an unmistakeable pale blue building. An assortment of Caribbean and ocean habitats is reproduced, with about 3,500 specimens of sea fauna.

The most spectacular is the one

with bottle-nosed dolphins, which are common in Cuban seas. Dolphin shows are performed at regular intervals. *The complex is open Tue–Sat 10am–6pm, with an entrance fee.*
You can either finish the tour here or continue your walk along the seafront to find a peaceful spot for sunbathing.

7 Playita 16

The water is clear, although swimming is not recommended because of the rocky shore. This is a good place to relax and enjoy the seaside location.

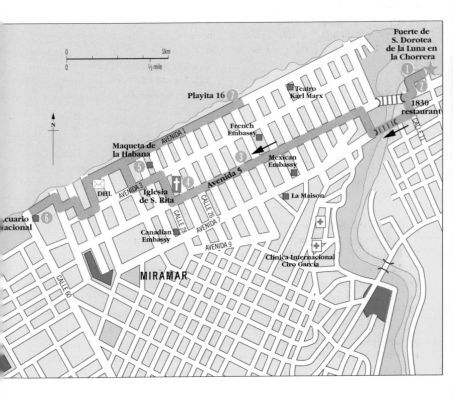

At various points during a typical stay in Havana, visitors will come across references to Ernest Hemingway, and there is in fact a tour that takes in the major sites of interest relating to this great American novelist. Ernest Hemingway's love affair with Cuba continued until his death in 1961. He was initially attracted by the marlin fishing, but soon gambling, prostitutes and cocktails were added to the list. He stayed in Hotel Ambos Mundos and was a regular at two bars nearby, the Bodequita del Medio and El Floridita. In 1940 he bought a 6-hectare (15-acre) farm outside Havana, called 'Finca la Vigía', in which he wrote some of his greatest novels. His staff included three gardeners, a cook and a man who tended the fighting cocks which Hemingway bred.

During the Second World War, he set up his own counter-intelligence unit with the aim of rooting out Nazi spies in Havana. He also armed his fishing boat, the *Pilar*, with bazookas and grenades, and his crew was made up of Cuban friends and Spanish exiles, as well as a

'This prize belongs to Cuba, since my works were created and conceived in Cuba, with the inhabitants of Cojímar, of which I am a citizen.' Cojímar was the fishing village and setting for the novel, and where he whiled away the evenings, trading stories, playing dominoes and drinking rum.

It was around this time that his drinking reached its peak. It is said that he would have whisky and cocktails during the day, followed by two bottles of wine at dinner, followed by absinthe and whisky with soda at various casinos until the early hours. It is believed that he helped to invent the *daquiri* cocktail.

radio operator supplied by the US Embassy. The boat cruised the waters around Havana searching for German U-boats. When it was apparent that these were unlikely to be found, the trips turned into a haze of drinking and fishing.

After the war, Hemingway wrote *The Old Man and the Sea*, which won him the Pulitzer Prize in 1953. In 1954 he won the Nobel Prize, and placed it at the foot of the Madonna del Cobre, near Santiago de Cuba, with the words:

When the political situation worsened around 1958 under Batista, Hemingway returned to his home in Idaho in the USA, from where he heard the news of Castro's victory. He returned to Cuba and made a public show of his support for the Revolution, and he later met Castro during a Marlin fishing tournament. In 1960 he left for Florida, committing suicide in 1961.

Facing page: Hemingway with Castro at a fishing competition
This page: Hemingway's boat *Pilar*

HAVANA EXCURSIONS

Day tours from Havana are plentiful and can be booked at the lobbies of most hotels. These are an ideal way of travelling outside Havana and seeing interesting sites without the worry of organising your own transport and guides. The tour bus will usually pick you up from your hotel and drop you back again afterwards. If you are staying in a *casa particular*, you can arrange pick-up from a nearby hotel.

Tours

While we have included a few of the more popular day trips from Havana, there are other tours which venture farther afield, for example to Viñales, Pinar del Rio, Trinidad and Cienfuegos.

These are generally best undertaken with an overnight stay, rather than trying to rush a visit within one day.

Jibacoa and Jaruco

Not usually included in tour brochures, Jibacoa is a pretty area within striking distance of Havana, being only 60km (37 miles) east of the city. It is well suited for snorkelling, as the reefs are close to the beach, and it is also a nice area for walking, as the hills extend down to the sea.

On the way back from Jibacoa, Jaruco makes an interesting diversion. From Santa Cruz del Norte, you can drive inland via the Central Camilo Cienfuegos to Jaruco, and 6km (3½ miles) to the west is the Parque Escaleras

The attractive beach at Jibacoa

de Jaruco. These *escaleras*, or stairs, are geological formations in the limestone, set in picturesque landscape.

Soroa

Soroa is a popular excursion that takes you to an area of natural beauty, containing a spa and resort in luxuriant hills. The biggest draw is the Orquideario (Orchid Garden), which is home to one of the largest orchid collections in the world. Containing more than 700 species of orchid, 250 of which are endemic, the garden was founded in 1943 by a lawyer from the Canary Islands, Tomás Felipe Camacho, and it has been declared a national monument.

The waterfall at Soroa

The *escaleras* (stairs) at Jaruco

The route from Havana to Soroa crosses a peaceful area of cultivated fields and rural villages, while Soroa itself lies 250m (820ft) above sea level in the middle of tropical forest. The area was named after two Basque brothers who owned most of the coffee plantations in the area, and the small town of Soroa contains a holiday village with good tourist facilities. One of the main attractions is the Salton, a spectacular waterfall on the Manantiales River.

Also of interest are the Mirador de Venus and Baños Romanos. You can park by the baths and walk up to the *mirador* (viewing spot), which gives fine views over the southern plains and forest-covered Sierra.

Sierra del Rosario, 81km (50 miles) southwest of the capital. Orchid Garden:

The Orchid Garden at Soroa

Tel: 852558. Open: daily 9am–4pm. Admission charge. Waterfall: 10-minute walk from the Villa Soroa. Admission fee. Mirador: 25-minute walk from the baths. Free if walking, a charge if going by horse.

Las Terrazas

A trip to the Biosphere Reserve at Las Terrazas is a very pleasant break from the bustle of Havana city, and illustrates the efforts the government has made to develop sustainable ecology which also attracts tourism.

There are two major coffee plantations usually visited by tours: La Victoria and Buenavista. The latter was developed by French settlers escaping the Haiti Revolution in the 19th Century. The colonial house has been restored, although the nearby slave barracks are in ruins.

The settlement at Las Terrazas was built in 1971 as a forestry and soil conservation station. Nearby slopes were terraced to prevent erosion and a large number of trees were planted to develop the area into an ecology reserve. As well as providing employment for local people, the area's sights attract a growing number of visitors. The Hotel Moka within the settlement is a beautiful Spanish colonial building, designed with ecological considerations in mind. There are bathing springs with cool, clear sulphur water nearby in the San Juan River, a delightful spot with small waterfalls, and deep pools surrounded by vegetation. There are changing facilities here too, so don't forget to take your bathing suit!

One of the many beaches along Varadero

Varadero

Sitting on the 19km (11¹/₂ miles) Península de Hicacos, Cuba's most important beach resort for package holidays, is also popular as a day excursion from Havana with tourists and locals alike. A typical day tour price will cost US$40–60 and takes roughly ten hours.

The bus journey takes slightly over two hours. However, a tour is better value than making your own way here. For a full description of the resort, *see p83*.

Coffee bean drying beds at an old coffee plantation

Western Cuba

Western Cuba is the area that most tourists focus on when they only have a limited amount of time in the country, after spending time in Havana and a beach resort such as Varadero. The area should not be missed, as it is one of outstanding natural beauty, with attractions and activities to suit a great variety of tastes.

A mogote (limestone outcrop)

The main attraction is the Viñales Valley, with an exotic landscape of limestone *mogotes* (outcrops), tobacco plantations, nature reserves, caves and mountains. In the far west, there is first-class scuba diving, as well as good beaches and ecotourist reserves.

The provincial towns and villages are quiet and agricultural, a far cry from the bustle of Havana, and the whole province offers a peaceful refuge from city sightseeing. It has always been a laid-back area, Pinar del Rio province being known as the least 'revolutionary' part of Cuba. Pinar del Río is also the area that produces the best tobacco in Cuba, and therefore in the world.

PINAR DEL RIO

The capital of the province is a lively and attractive town, and gives visitors a good taste of provincial Cuba. So named because of the many pine groves in the area, it has many neoclassical buildings with columns, as well as distinctive red tiles on the roofs of many houses.

Cigar factory

A visit to the cigar factory is included in most tours of the area. This tiny factory, which reputedly makes the best cigars in the world, is housed in a former 19th-century hospital, and visitors can watch workers sitting at desks, rolling leaves of dried tobacco and making *veguero* cigars, which are not exported. Don't be surprised if some workers secretly try to sell you some! *'Fabrica de Tabacos Francisco Donatien', Calle Maceo 157 Oeste. Tel: 823424. Open: Mon–Fri, and Sat am. Admission charge if not part of a tour. Cameras and bags are not allowed in the factory.*

Palacio de Guasch

A somewhat extravagant building, this has an unusual façade consisting of Moorish arches, Gothic spires and even

Palacio de Guasch, Pinar del Río

Province of Pinar del Rio

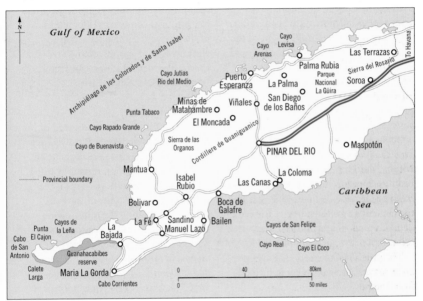

Baroque elements. It was built in 1909 for a wealthy physician who wanted to reproduce the favourite architectural styles that inspired him during his travels. Now the building is a natural history museum.
Calle Martí, corner of Comandante Pinares. Museum: Tel: 823087. Open: Mon–Sat 8am–5pm. Admission charge.

THE SIERRA DEL ROSARIO

Now a UNESCO world biosphere reserve, the Sierra del Rosario mountain range covers the eastern part of Pinar del Rio province, including a 250sq km (97 sq miles) biosphere reserve.

Soroa

Please refer to the Soroa section within the Havana excursions chapter (*see p73*).

81km (50 miles) southwest of Havana, in the Sierra del Rosario. Can be driven from the capital either directly from the autopista, and driving northwest from Candelaria, or by going 18km (11 miles) west from Havana, then southeast from Moka through the Sierra del Rosario.

Las Terrazas

Please refer to the Las Terrazas section within the Havana excursions chapter (*see p74*).

51km (31 miles) west of Havana, and 4km (2¹/₂ miles) north of the autopista (motorway), in the Sierra del Rosario.

VIÑALES

Although just a small town, Viñales is delightful, more pleasant to stay in than the much larger Pinar del Rio. It sits in a dramatic valley in the Sierra de los Organos, so called because Spanish sailors centuries ago caught sight of the profiles of *mogotes* through the fog, and it reminded them of a church organ. The town is now maintained by the government as an example of a well-preserved colonial settlement. The main street is lined with trees and wooden colonnades, and with red-tiled buildings typical of the area. The main square, Parque Martí has recently been beautifully restored, as has the Iglesia del Sagrado Corazón de Jesús. Built in 1888, the church is now the home of the Casa de la Cultura, and includes an art gallery.

25km (15 miles) north of Pinar del Río in the Valle de Viñales. Nearby are two very good hotels: Hotel La Ermita and Hotel Los Jazmines.

THE VIÑALES VALLEY

This valley, which has been declared a national monument, and is characterised by huge limestone outcrops, is worth at least a day's

MOGOTES

Mogotes are limestone outcrops that resemble sugar loaves. They are some of the most ancient rocks in Cuba, and are the remains of what was once a limestone plateau. The soft limestone was eroded from the inside while hard limestone pillars remained with ancient caves within them. Although many have thick vegetation growing on them, there is often very little soil, with a number of endemic plant species growing here, including the corch palm and mountain palm tree.

visit, and a stay overnight in the area is recommended to fully enjoy the scenery. Many tourist companies offer a tour of the area which includes a visit to cigar and rum factories, enjoying a spectacular view of the area at Hotel Jazmines, and a visit to caves.

Cueva del Indio

This beautiful cave was discovered in 1920, although lighting was only added in the 1950s. The first part of the tour here is on foot through tunnels, while a small motorboat takes visitors on the underground river (part of the San Vicente) through to the other side, about 0.4km (¼ mile) away.

6km (3½ miles) north of Viñales. Try and avoid the rush between 11.30am and 2.30pm, when many tour parties visit. Admission charge when not part of a tour. There is a restaurant within walking distance, where tour groups are given a simple country lunch.

Gran Caverna de Santo Tomás

This is the largest network of caves in the whole of Latin America, with 18km (11 miles) of galleries and up to five levels of grottoes. In days gone by, the largest, the Cueva del Salon, was used by local farmers for festivals, but it is not normally open for tourists.

El Moncada, 17km (10½ miles) west of Viñales. Charge for cave walk and guide.

Mural de la Prehistoria

Although not to everyone's taste, this mural is on a grand scale, being painted on the face of a *mogote* (limestone outcrop), and it receives many visitors. It was painted by Lovigildo González,

Torch ginger

a pupil of the famous Mexican painter Diego Rivera, in 1962, and it depicts the history of evolution from ammonites to *Homo sapiens*.
2km (1 mile) west of Viñales, by the Mogote Dos Hermanos. Open: daily 8am–7pm. Admission charge.

THE WEST COAST

More effort is required to visit the Guanahacabibes Peninsula, which forms the western tip of Cuba, but it is well worth it if you are interested in either diving or nature. The peninsula was named after a Pre-Columbian ethnic group. It consists of a strip of land 100km (60 miles) long and up to 34km (20¹/₂ miles) wide, and it was declared a world biosphere reserve in 1985, with the aim of protecting the flora and fauna.

Guanahacabibes National Park

A paradise for keen naturalists, the park contains 12 species of amphibian, 19 reptiles including iguanas, 10 mammals, and 147 bird species, including woodpeckers, parrots and hummingbirds. There are fossil coastlines, caves and blue holes, while the forest is made up of a mix of deciduous and evergreen trees. The

area is slowly gearing itself up to cater for ecotourists.
The park is at the far southwestern tip of Cuba. La Bajada is the nearby scientific station and community. Access to the inner zone is limited. Permits for entering can be obtained in Pinar del Rio at tourist offices within hotels, and visits to the park are made in jeeps with a local guide.

María la Gorda

Reputedly the best diving centre in Cuba, María la Gorda is relatively isolated, but visitors will be rewarded with beautiful coral reefs, warm translucent sea and a real tropical aquarium. The reefs are easy to reach, lying just a short distance from the shore.

The name of the place originates from a legend about a plump (*gorda*) girl called Maria. She was abducted by pirates on the Venezuelan coast and abandoned here, and was then forced to sell herself to passing buccaneers in order to survive.

Areas of particular interest to divers include the so-called Black Coral Valley, a wall of coral over 100m (328ft) long, and the Salon de María, a sea cave 18m (59ft) deep, which is home to rare species of fish.

The dive boat usually goes a short distance to dive sites, mostly reef or wall dives. Fish in the area include rays, turtles, reef and whale sharks, and barracuda. There is also good snorkelling, with small coral heads close to the white sand beach.
12km (7 miles) south of La Bajada. María la Gorda Diving Centre, La Bajada. Tel: 8278131. Package tours can be arranged in Havana from Cubamar and Puertosol.

Cuban cigars

Cigars are integral to Cuba's culture and identity, and they are one of the country's abiding symbols. They are perhaps the most popular and sought-after souvenirs for tourists, and understandably so, because Cuba produces the finest cigars in the world. It is said that, just before he ordered the full trade embargo on Cuba in 1961, President Kennedy secretly ordered supplies of Cuban cigars to be bought for his personal use.

The origins of Cuban cigars begin with the native Indians who used tobacco (*cohiba*) during religious rites to invoke the gods. Columbus noted the natives' habit of smoking roughly rolled dried leaves during his second journey to the New World. The Spaniards soon acquired the taste for tobacco, and by the 17th century it was traded in the European market, being thought to have therapeutic qualities. Tobacco plantations were first established near the Rio Almendares (now Havana), in the centre of the island, and later on in the west of the island. By the 19th century, tobacco planters and merchants were very prosperous.

Nowadays, tobacco is cultivated in the provinces of Pinar del Rio, Villa Clara, Sancti Spíritus, Granma and Santiago de Cuba. It is a very labour-intensive process. Seedlings are transplanted from the nursery between October and December, and weeded after two weeks. Harvesting takes place from January to March, when the leaves are

collected by hand, starting from the bottom of the plant. The leaves are hung up to dry until they turn yellow and then reddish-gold, which normally takes about 50 days. After the first fermentation of 30 days, the leaves are stripped of the main vein, dampened and packed for the second fermentation period of 60 days. Then, after a storage and ageing period of months or even years, they are rolled by teams of factory workers sitting at desks. A skilled factory worker makes an average of 120 cigars a day, equipped with a *chaveta* knife, a guillotine and a pot of gum. *Torcedores* (cigar rollers) are highly skilled, often coming from generations of artisans.

Different types of leaves are used in the rolling of a cigar. The core of the cigar is made up of filler leaves, called *tripa*, which are chosen to obtain a particular flavour. Next is the *capote*, the binder leaf that keeps the core compact. Finally, the wrapper leaf (the *capa*) is rolled on the outside and gives the cigar its smooth, velvety appearance. After wrapping, the cigar is trimmed and then measured to gauge against various standard sizes in terms of length and diameter.

Cigars are made in different shapes and sizes. Heavy cigars tend to have a fuller flavour compared to standard or slim cigars, while some are tapered (*figurado*). There are 32 brands of Cuban cigars, all of which have famous and often historic designs from the 19th century. Cohiba cigars have been produced for the international market since 1966 and tend to be the mildest, while Montecristo is one of the oldest brands, dating from 1935.

Care must be taken when buying cigars. Do not be tempted to buy them on the street, as these are likely to be low-quality fakes. Always buy from a state-run shop, and check that the box is sealed with a four-language warranty. On the bottom should be a stamp saying '*Habanos S.A. Hecho en Cuba totalmente a mano*'. The cigars should be tightly rolled, with no lumps, and nothing should come out if you turn them upside down.

Facing page: a *guajiro* (smallholder's cottage) located amid fields of tobacco
This page: cigar maker at work

Western Central Cuba

The Western Central section of Cuba consists of three provinces: Matanzas, Cienfuegos and Villa Clara. They are the rural heart of the island, with a gentle landscape and cultivated fields which you will see if travelling from Havana to Trinidad or further east. How much of this area tourists see depends very much on the time available to them. For one- or two-week holidays, tourists based in Havana or Varadero might only get as far as Trinidad, but there is so much more to see if you have more time.

A mangrove swamp

Provinces of Matanzas, Villa Clara and Cienfuegos

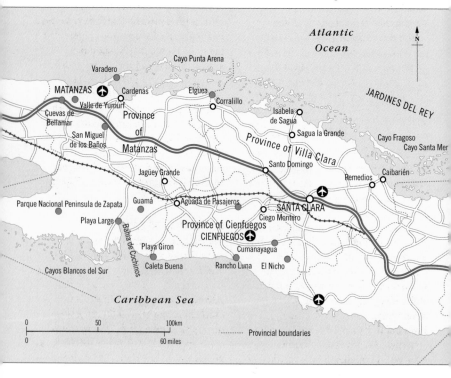

Atlantic Ocean

N

Cayo Punta Arena

Varadero

MATANZAS   Cardenas   Elguea

Valle de Yumurí   Corralillo   JARDINES DEL REY

Cuevas de   Province   Isabela
Bellamar   de Sagua

San Miguel   of   Sagua la Grande
de los Baños   Cayo Fragoso

                Matanzas   Province of Villa Clara   Cayo Santa Mer

        Jagüey Grande   Santo Domingo   Caibarién

Parque Nacional Peninsula de Zapata   Guamá   Remedios

        Playa Large   Aguada de Pasajeros   SANTA CLARA

                                Ciego Montero

                Province of Cienfuegos

Playa Giron   CIENFUEGOS

                    Cumanayagua
Caleta Buena   Rancho Luna   El Nicho

Cayos Blancos del Sur

Caribbean Sea

0   50   100km
0   60 miles

·········· Provincial boundaries

Putting the famous holiday resort of Varadero to one side, there are the lively cities of Santa Clara and Cienfuegos, and to the south are the beautiful nature reserves in the Zapata Peninsula, a must for nature lovers and for anyone who wants to venture beyond city sightseeing and beaches.

From the mid 16th century, both coasts in this region were regularly raided by pirates for the best part of 200 years. Santa Clara was founded as a result of families moving inland, while Cienfuegos was founded 150 years later by settlers from the former French colonies of Haita and Louisiana.

VARADERO

Cuba's chief beach resort has long been both popular and exclusive, illustrated by the fact that the 19km (11½ miles) Península de Hicacos on which the resort sits, is connected to the mainland by a drawbridge. The only Cubans that tourists will meet in Varadero work in the tourist industry. It is therefore very safe, comfortable and sanitised. To be honest, staying in an all-inclusive resort in Varadero, wearing a coloured wristband, gives tourists zero exposure to the real Cuba – one could be at any international resort in the world.

Development of the peninsula did not really begin until the early 20th century, when some families from nearby Cardenas built themselves summer residences on the peninsula. Varadero is still undergoing large-scale development, mostly with foreign investors in joint-ventures. Capacity is expected to reach 30,000 rooms, although it remains to be seen whether

it becomes over-developed. It is a good place for a family beach holiday, as long as the focus is on water sports and resort activities, rather than sightseeing. Organised excursions are available for those wishing to see something of the real Cuba.

The peninsula is a succession of hotel villages with shops, cinemas, sports centres and nightlife venues. It can be explored by bicycle although there is little of historical or architectural interest. The southern end of the resort is more downmarket, while the northern end has more international-class luxury hotels.

There are a few tourist sites on the peninsula. The Museo Municipal recounts the history of Varadero, housed in a white and blue wooden chalet from the early 1900s. Villa Xanadu is a sumptuous mansion with golf course and gardens, built in 1929 by the American chemical engineer Alfred Dupont, and now houses Restaurante Las Americas, the most elegant in Varadero. Nature lovers should visit Punta Hicacos, a nature reserve with some attractive features, and Parque Josone, a beautiful park with a rowing lake.

PENÍNSULA DE ZAPATA

Visitors come to this area of Cuba for a number of specific reasons, making it different from other tourist centres on the island. The peninsula's main attractions include a wildlife park, excellent facilities for water sports and diving, and the Bay of Pigs invasion site.

The peninsula itself is one of the least populated on the island, consisting mostly of a huge swamp partly covered by forest. However, this swamp forms one of the most complete wildlife reserves in the Caribbean, making it a magnet for nature lovers. The area around Laguna del Tesoro has been designated a national park, the Gran Parque Nacional de Montemar, and it is the largest ecosystem on the island. Here one can walk among unspoilt nature and luxurious vegetation, look at mangroves, swamp plants, and birds with multicoloured plumage. For the more cautious tourist, do not worry; there are no poisonous snakes or other scary animals on the island!

Bahía de Cochinos

Bahía de Cochinos (Bay of Pigs) is in fact the name for the large bay, which includes a number of beaches and sights, including Playa Larga, Caleta de Rosario and la Cueva de los Peces. Visitors to the bay come mainly to visit the Bay of Pigs invasion site and to take advantage of excellent places for snorkelling and diving.

Playa Girón

Playa Girón is on the eastern side of the bay, and is home to the Museo Girón, which commemorates the famous battle which took place here in 1961. It was named after a French pirate from the

Península de Zapata

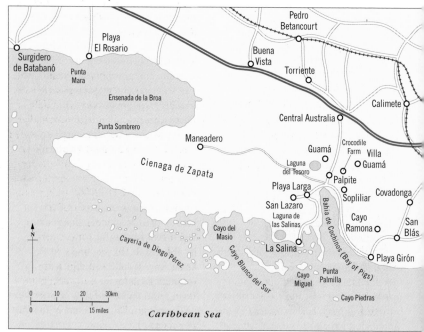

17th century who found refuge here. The museum covers the invasion using documents and photos, a tank and weapons, as well as films taken during the invasion.

Museo Girón, Playa Girón, Península de Zapata. Tel: 4122. Open: daily 9am–12pm and 1–5pm. Admission charge.

Playa Larga

Playa Larga is a good base to explore the area and is also a popular resort with Cubans, as the beach is better than most along this part of the coast. Thick vegetation grows almost as far as the shore, although the resort area is better, with hotels and good facilities.

BAY OF PIGS INVASION

This beach is best known as the site of the decisive battle between Fidel Castro's revolutionary forces and the invading US-backed Cuban exiles, which took place at the height of the Cold War. On April 17, 1961, 1,400 Cuban exiles trained by the CIA landed on Cuban soil with the aim of overthrowing Castro's regime, supported by US air force planes, which bombed the island's air bases. They were met by Fidel Castro's forces as well as volunteers from the local population, which stopped the invasion in its tracks.

It was a controversial point in history, not only because it briefly threatened the newly born Cuban Revolution, but also because it was a humiliation for President Kennedy's presidency, and proved that the Revolution had won the hearts and minds of the Cuban people.

The coral reef offshore offers excellent dive sites. Around the bay to the east is Cueva de los Peces, a natural pool 70m (230ft) deep, full of fish and popular for diving and snorkelling.

The Laguna del Tesoro

This 9-sq km (3½-sq miles) lagoon is over 10m (33ft) deep and an important home for flocks of migrating birds. Coming from the north, you soon reach Boca de Guamá.

Criadero de Crocodilos

The crocodile farm is situated at the Zapata Tourist Institute, the biggest farm of its kind on the island. Founded in 1962, it safeguards 16 endangered species of reptile. This is a popular stop for tour buses, so facilities are excellent.

Open: daily 9am–4.30pm. Admission charge.

Villa Guamá

A holiday village with a difference is the best way to describe this series of eco-friendly huts. Situated in the middle of the lagoon, this is a replica Amerindian village where visitors can stay in wooden thatched huts with modern amenities such as air-conditioning. The huts are supported on stilts and are connected to one another by hanging bridges and canoes. This is an ideal place for birdwatchers to spend a night or two, and the village has tourist facilities, including a restaurant, museum and even a disco! Insect repellent is recommended for staying overnight.

Boats are available to take you from Boca de Guamá to Villa Guamá for a fee. The journey takes one hour.

Santa Clara

Many tourists visit Santa Clara primarily to see the monumental Che Guevara mausoleum and sites related to the Cuban Revolution, in which Santa Clara played a decisive role. It is also used as a stopover city because it is central to the main tourist destinations on the island. While it is a pleasant university town, it does not have the same architectural history as Camagüey or Santiago de Cuba.

Monument to Che Guevara

Santa Clara was founded in 1689 by people moving inland to escape pirate raids on the coast, but it was in 1958 that the town was made famous, when it gained its reputation as 'city of the heroic guerilla'.

Memorial Comandante Ernesto Che Guevara

One of the most popular sites in the country for Cubans to visit, this monument in the Plaza de la Revolución was built in 1988 to commemorate the 30th anniversary of the battle of Santa Clara. The memorial is dominated by the famous bronze statue of Che with his arm in plaster (he had broken it during the battle), by sculptor José Delarra. Under the monument is a Mausoleum and the Museo Histórica de la Revolución, which has some of Che's personal belongings on display. *Plaza de la Revolución Ernesto Che Guevara. Tel: 5878. Open: Tue–Sat 8am– 9pm, Sun 8am–6pm. Admission charge. Numbers allowed in the mausoleum at any one time are limited to 20.*

BATTLE OF SANTA CLARA

Che Guevara's forces had already defeated government forces to gain control of the city the day before, when dictator Batista sent an armoured train with soldiers and supplies to reinforce Santiago de Cuba. Guevara and his limited number of men ambushed the train, causing the surrender of the troops, a decisive battle which lead to Batista fleeing the country. The train in question is now a tourist attraction and the remains of Che Guevara are interred in the mausoleum at the site of this greatest victory.

Monumento a la Toma del Tren Blindado

The historic ambush of Batista's troop train is commemorated in this museum-monument, on the spot where it took place. Four carriages have been preserved, as well as the bulldozer used to cause the derailment of the train, and other memorabilia. Overlooking the site is the hill El Capiro, where Che and his troops waited for the train. There are excellent views from here over the city.

Parque Leoncio Vidal

This charming park is in the heart of the city with flower beds, wrought-iron benches and period street lamps from the 1920s. The plaza's charm makes it a popular place for residents to stroll, both day and night, and some of the buildings around the square have been renovated and turned into hotels. The park was named after the colonel in the national independence army who was killed in battle in the square in 1896.

Until 1894, the square was racially segregated, with blacks having to walk around the outside areas of the park. *Between Calles Marta Abreu, Colon and Cuba.*

Teatro de la Caridad

The austere exterior of this late 19th-century theatre belies the beautifully ornate interior, which has painted panels and chandeliers. The name 'charity theatre' came from the offering of additional services such as a restaurant, barber, ballroom and gambling, which collected money for the poor of the city. The theatre itself is most interesting, with wrought-iron balusters and some folding seats (a new innovation in Cuba at the time), as well as a beautifully frescoed ceiling by the Spanish artist Camilo Salaya. *Parque Vidal 3. Tel: 5548.*

Parque Leoncio Vidal, Santa Clara

Che Guevara

Without doubt, Che Guevara is the Cuban Revolution's greatest hero and his iconic status is due perhaps as much to his photogenic looks and charismatic personality as to his extraordinary leadership qualities and courage in the field of battle. He believed in a revolutionary society based on moral rather than material wealth, and defended Third World rights with great eloquence.

Ernesto Guevara was born in Argentina, acquiring the nickname 'Che' after an Argentinian figure of speech.

Initially a medical student, he started his personal struggle against imperialism in Guatemala at the time the CIA toppled the elected government, and he met Fidel Castro in Mexico soon afterwards. He joined Fidel's group of rebels in the run-up to the guerilla struggle against Batista's dictatorship, and was a key commander in the military success of the Revolution in 1959. His greatest moment was the capture of Santa Clara and the successful ambush, in December 1958, of Batista's troop and munitions train. This subsequently resulted in Batista fleeing the country and victory for the Revolution. Guevara took the position of head of the Central Bank and the Ministry of Industry, overseeing a period of chaotic economic reforms.

Guevara's role in the new government was not successful and he became disillusioned, leaving for the Congo and then Bolivia to join the guerilla struggles there. In 1967 he was captured by CIA-backed government troops and executed in Bolivia.

In 1997, on the 30th anniversary of his death, the body of Che Guevara was returned to Cuba and interred in a bronze mausoleum in Santa Clara. He remains one of only two foreigners in the history of the island to be proclaimed a Cuban citizen 'by birth'; the other was Dominican Maximo Gómez, the general in the Wars of Independence.

Facing page: the enigmatic Che Guevara

KORDA'S PHOTO

Alberto Diaz Gutierrez could never have imagined that one of the magazine photos that he took of Che Guevara, rejected by the newspaper *Revolución*, would become famous.

The son of a railway worker, the young fashion photographer took the name 'Korda' because he thought that it sounded like 'Kodak' and would therefore be better for business. When he was 31, an expedition into the countryside showed him the reality of peasant life with its grinding poverty; he became a revolutionary, and photographer for the revolutionary leadership. His famous photograph of Che was taken in 1960 at the funeral of a Cuban merchant seaman killed in a sabotaged munitions ship.

A huge poster of the photo was used as a backdrop for Fidel Castro's speech in Plaza de la Revolución that paid homage to Che upon his death in 1967. The global coverage of the event catapulted the image, and Che, to iconic status. It has subsequently been used on everything from T-shirts and posters to advertisements.

The photo was used without permission, and Korda did nothing about his copyright or possible royalties for ten years. It was only in 1998 that Korda sued and won damages following the use of the photo in yet another advertising campaign. He donated the money to the Cuba health service because he believed that Che would have done the same.

Korda died in 2001 at the age of 73.

Cienfuegos

Despite being surrounded by industry and unspectacular scenery, the maritime town of Cienfuegos has a well-preserved charm and some fascinating architectural gems, as well as a captivating bay. While it is a historic town, it also has a well-to-do feel to it. Well worth visiting on the outskirts are the magnificent botanical gardens and the aquarium, which are often on the itinerary of tour buses to Cienfuegos.

Avoiding the midday sun in Cienfuegos

The Paseo del Prado, the main thoroughfare in Cienfuegos

The small province of Cienfuegos is largely low lying, with an emphasis on sugar plantations, sugar being the mainstay for the town's wealth, along with cattle. The diving is also good along the coast.

Founded in 1819, the town was named after the first Cuban Governor General at the time, José Cienfuegos. As one of the few towns in Cuba founded by the French rather than the Spanish, it has an interesting blend of architectural styles. The town was planned in a geometric layout following neoclassical guidelines. In the colonial era, it was named 'pearl of the south', due to the beauty of the town and bay. There are many legends here about pirates, and the fortress was built by the Spanish in 1745 as a result of the threat of attack.

The town centre

Cienfuegos has a comfortable, relaxed atmosphere, partly due to the bustle in the streets, especially the pedestrianised main shopping street (Avenida 54, known as the Boulevard), which seems to have more shops than in other Cuban towns. The other main street in the town is Paseo del Prado (Calle 37), which has a central promenade for people to stroll along or sit.

It is the liveliest thoroughfare in the city, established in 1922, flanked by elegant, well-preserved buildings, with monuments in the centre honouring the great and the good.

Catedral de la Purísima Concepción

One of the major buildings around Parque Marti is the Cathedral of Cienfuegos, with two bell towers of different heights, and a neoclassical façade. Built in 1869, it has stained-glass windows made in France and a neo-Gothic interior with silvered columns.
Avenida 56, on the east side of Calle 29. Tel: 5297. Open: Mon–Fri 7am–3pm, Sat 7am–12pm & 2–4pm, Sun 7am–12pm.

Museo Provincial

Formerly the casino, this eclectic-style building opened in 1896. Now the Provincial Museum, it houses period objects and furniture reflecting the great wealth of the leading families of the area in the 19th century. There are also two rooms of contemporary art.
South side of Parque Marti, on Avenida 54. Tel: 9722. Open: Tue–Sat 10am–6pm, Sun 9am–1pm. Admission charge.

Palacio de Ferrer

This is a beautiful early 19th-century building of eclectic architecture, with a distinctive cupola, situated on the west side of Parque Marti. Although the interior is sadly neglected, it still has impressive marble floors, staircases and walls, and Italian ceramic wall tiles, that hint at the grandeur of past times. There are some rusty spiral steps going up the tower for some great views of the area. It is now the Casa de la Benjamín Duarte, but was originally built by the sugar magnate José Ferrer.
Avenida 54 corner of Calle 25, on the west side of Parque Marti. Tel: 6584. Open: Mon–Sat 8.30am–7pm. Voluntary admission charge.

Parque Marti

Formerly the Plaza de Armas, this square is vast, with many buildings of historical importance surrounding it. As a result, it has been declared a national monument. It was here in 1819 that the city was founded in a solemn ceremony under a hibiscus tree. In the middle of the park is the 'zero kilometre', the central point marking the middle of Cienfuegos. It is a very pleasant park, with a rotunda bandstand, benches and a statue of José Martí at one end. The arch on the west side of the square is the only triumphal arch in Cuba, symbolising the entrance to the city, and commissioned in 1902 by the workers' corporation. One side of the square is taken up by the provincial government assembly building, the Palacio del Ayuntamiento. The buildings around the square are mostly in an excellent state of repair, making a popular stopping point for tours.

Teatro Tomás Terry

A masterpiece of 19th-century architecture, this theatre was built in 1889 to fulfil the last will of the Venezuelan sugar magnate and former mayor Tomás Terry Adams, with the proceeds of a donation by his family. The Italian-style building is a beautifully preserved, charming two-tiered auditorium. There is a lovely fresco by Camilo Salaya, a Spanish painter, and world-famous performers such as Enrico Caruso and Sarah Bernhardt performed here in the 1900s. Two sets of theatre boxes nearest the stage were traditionally reserved for mourners who did not want to be seen by the rest of the audience, and who could enter and leave the theatre through a separate door.

Avenida 56 (San Carlos), overlooking Parque Martí. Tel: 3361. Open: daily 9am–6pm. Charge for admission and guided tour.

Out of town
Castillo de Jagua

This majestic military structure was the third most important fortress on the island in the 18th century. It served the important purpose of protecting the region from Jamaican pirates. Legend has it that a mysterious lady ghost used to walk the corridors of the citadel each night, frightening the guards.

The fortress currently includes a restaurant that specialises in fish dishes. *Poblado Castillo de Jagua, 29km (18 miles) south of the town. Tel: 6402. Ferries to the fortress available from Avenida 46 in Cienfuegos harbour or Pasacaballos Hotel. Open: daily 8am–5pm. Admission charge.*

Jardín Botánico de Cienfuegos

Outside of Cienfuegos, but well worth a special trip or detour, is the city's botanical garden, which is one of the largest in Latin America at 90 hectares (222 acres), and which is now a national monument. It is also known as Jardín Botánico Soledad, named after the original owner of the Soledad sugar works, Edwin Atkins. It has more than 2,000 different species of plant, including 300 types of palm trees. Of special interest are a gigantic Banyan tree with aerial roots and a circumference of over 20m (66ft), and the many specimens of cacti in the greenhouse. *23km (14 miles) east of Cienfuegos, between the villages of San Antón and Guaos. Tel: 45326. Open: daily 8am–5pm.*

Admission charge. Guides are only in Spanish; tips are welcomed!

Palacio de Valle

Normally included in city tours, this is the most striking and original building for miles around. Now a restaurant, it is almost obscenely lavish in its decoration. The palace was built in 1917 by one of the wealthiest men in Cuba at the time, the sugar merchant Acisclo del Valle Blanco, and subsequently became a casino in dictator Batista's time.

The two-storey building is decorated with Gothic, Venetian and neo-Moorish styles and was inspired by the owner's travels in Europe, especially Moorish Spain.
Calle 37 between Avenida 0 and 2, Punta Gorda. Tel: 451226. Open: daily 9.30am–11pm. Admission charge.

The extravagant Palacio de Valle

Trinidad

Arriving in Trinidad is like experiencing a time warp that takes you back to colonial times. The perfectly preserved buildings and cobbled streets result from the town's isolation from the rest of Cuba for 100 years, and its position as a UNESCO World Heritage Site. Skilful restoration of sections of the town has succeeded in breathing fresh life into Trinidad.

Palacio Brunet

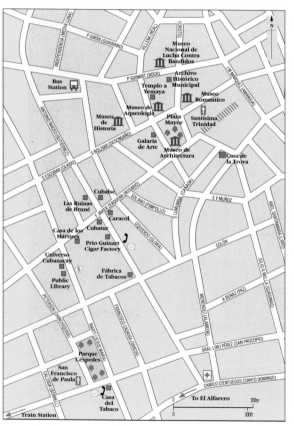

Some describe Trinidad as Cuba's most important town after Havana in terms of tourism and architecture. Certainly the growing popularity of the town is reflected in the number of tourists wandering the streets. The city was founded in 1514 by Diego Velázquez, and was a major trade centre in the 17th and 18th centuries, especially in sugar and slaves. Many of the town's museums are housed in the old residences of the wealthy landowners of this time.

By the mid 19th century, Trinidad went into decline, mainly because of the Industrial Revolution in Europe which powered the production of sugar beet. As a result, Trinidad became frozen in time until the 1950s.

Visitors coming here from Havana find it a welcome change from the bustle and grandeur of the capital's streets. Trinidad is a quaint, easy-going town with cobblestone streets and pastel-coloured houses, and worth at least two days' stay. It is also an ideal base from which to explore nearby towns such as Cienfuegos and Santa Clara, and for exploring the picturesque countryside of rolling hills, waterfalls and beaches.

STREET NAMES IN TRINIDAD

The names of Trinidad's streets are confusing, as each has an old name and a new one, pre- and post-Cuban Revolution. The old ones have been painted over in white but are still legible. There is some debate among locals as to which they prefer; many like the old names, although it would be inappropriate to speak against the new revolutionary names in public.

Colonial house in Trinidad

Plaza Mayor, Trinidad

Plaza Mayor lies at the heart of the town, and many of the principal museums and buildings face this square, making it easy to see most of the city's sights in a day. The benches in the square are a perfect place to relax in the shade of the palms and watch the colourful buildings around you change hue as the sun loses its strength in the late afternoon.

Plaza Mayor

Iglesia y Convento de San Francisco

One block west of Plaza Mayor lies this monastery, symbol of the town, with fine views from its bell tower. The building was originally used by Franciscan monks in 1813, but it has subsequently been used as a garrison for the Spanish army, a school, and is now home to the Museo de la Lucha Contra Bandidos, exhibiting photos and memorabilia from the campaign against counter-revolutionaries in the Escambray Mountains in the 1960s.
Calle Hernández, corner of Guinart. Tel: 4121. Open: Tue and Fri 9am–10pm, Wed, Thur, Sat, Sun 9am–5pm. Admission charge.

Iglesia Parroquial de Santísima Trinidad

This is the largest church in Cuba, dominating the Plaza Mayor. Famous for its acoustics, the highlights of this late 19th-century church are the beautiful carved wooden altars made of precious woods. Also impressive is the statue of Senor de la Vera Cruz ('Lord of the True Cross'), made in Spain and intended for Mexico, but its journey was disrupted three times by strong winds that blew the ship back to Trinidad. The decision to leave part of the cargo behind, including the statue, was seen as a sign from heaven, and the statue has been worshipped since then. The Christ of Veracruz is the patron saint of Trinidad.
East side of Plaza Mayor. Open: daily 11.30am–1pm. Mass daily at 8–9pm, from which tourists are excluded.

Museo de Architectura Colonial

This pretty colonial mansion on the east of the square is the only museum of its kind in Cuba, covering different architectural styles in the town and illustrating colonial building techniques. The building was the residence of the Sánchez Iznaga family in the 18th century, who made their money from sugar. It has slim columns, wooden beams and a pretty portico, and one of the highlights is a 19th-century version of a shower with an array of pipes for hot and cold water.
South side of Plaza Mayor. Tel: 3208. Open: Sun–Thur, Sat 9am–5pm. Admission charge.

18th-century shower

Palacio Brunet (Museo Romántico)

Perhaps the most attractive museum in the town, the Museo Romántico has an impressive collection of ornaments, furniture and paintings in the Romantic style. The objects complement the building well, which was owned, as always in Trinidad, by a wealthy local businessman, in this case the Conde de Brunet and his family (called Borrel), who owned the house in the mid-19th century and made his fortune from cattle and sugar. When he died, his properties included two sugar mills and 700 slaves. Locals often use the Museo Romántico as a setting for wedding photos.
Northeast corner of Plaza Mayor, next to the Church of Santísima Trinidad.

Tel: 4363. Open: Tue–Sun 9am–5pm. Admission charge.

Palacio Cantero (Museo Histórico)

As well as having a commanding view of the historic town centre, this museum also exhibits items recounting the history of the region with historical, cultural and scientific displays. The sumptuous 19th-century building is neoclassical in style, and the frescoed entrance hall, in particular, is wonderful, making the museum popular with tour parties.
Calle Bolívar 423. Tel: 4460. Open: Sun–Thur, Sat 9am–5pm. Admission charge.

Plaza Mayor with Palacio Brunet

Walk: Plaza Mayor, Trinidad

The area around Plaza Mayor is so small that a tour will not involve much walking – instead, the effort will be in absorbing the history of Trinidad and avoiding tripping up on the cobblestones, which are uneven. Thankfully the pavements are flat!

Allow 2 hours.

Although relatively short, you may find this walk tiring due to the heat of the sun. Keep in the shade as much as possible and remember to take regular breaks for drinks at the bars dotted around the square! For example, there is a picturesque outdoor bar up the steps on the right-hand side of the Iglesia Parroquial de la Santisima Trinidad, and there is often a band playing there to keep you entertained. The logical starting point for the walk is in Plaza Mayor, under the shade of the palm trees.

1 Museo de Architectura Colonial

An introduction to the architecture of Trinidad will be useful at this first port of call. The Casa de los Sánchez Iznaga is also a beautiful example of the kind of restoration that is typical in Trinidad.

Walk downhill across the square, past the yellow Casa de Aldemán Ortiz, turn left and walk one block down Bolívar then turn right.

2 Palacio Cantero

Now the Museo Histórico, this is worth a visit not only for the exhibits on the history of the region, but also for the great views to be had from the tower.

Walk back uphill on Bolívar, and take a left along Villena.

3 Plazuela del Jigüe

This tiny area in front of the El Jigue restaurant is where the first mass in Trinidad was celebrated in 1514, beneath the acacia (*jigüe*) tree. Notice the lovely painted tiles on the outside of the porticoed restaurant.

Just up from this square is a blue building with a few steps up to the door.

4 Canchánchara

A quaint *casa de infusiones* with lovely shaded tables outside, this *casa* is famous for the cocktail of the same name, made with rum, sugar, honey, lime and water, and served in an earthenware pot. An ideal spot to sample a refreshing *canchánchara* and listen to traditional music.

Once out of the building, turn left and left again, walking uphill on Guinart to the corner.

5 Iglesia y Convento de San Francisco

The church bell tower is the symbol of the city and offers fine views of the town. This monastery is home to the Museo de la Lucha Contra Bandidos.

Walk towards Plaza Mayor along

Echerri and look for the yellow building on your left.

6 Palacio Brunet

The Museo Romántico has an impressive collection of furniture and other items that belonged to the Borrel family. It is easy to imagine the lifestyle of the wealthy local families who resided in this type of mansion, and there are beautiful views from the upper-floor balconies.

Further along Echerri is the church.

7 Iglesia Parroquial de la Santísima Trinidad

Built in the late 19th century, the Church of the Holy Trinity has a beautiful carved wooden altar and is the largest church in Cuba.

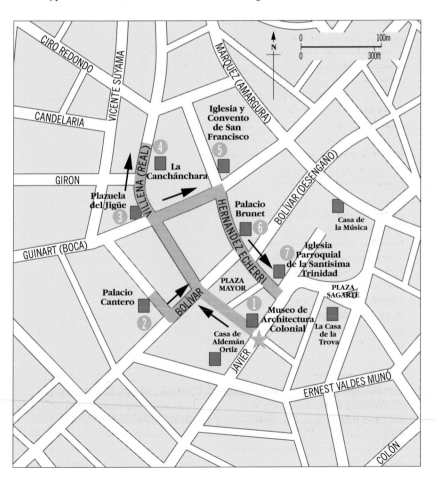

Other Trinidad sights and excursions

Ermita de Nuestra Señora de la Candelaria de la Popa

Visitors wanting a view of the city from the nearby hill will walk past this small church via a narrow, steep street from Plaza Mayor. Although closed, it is in a beautiful location. Damaged by a cyclone in 1812, the three-arch bell tower was added later. The walk further uphill takes you to a television transmission tower from which there are great views across the area.

Motel Las Cuevas

This hillside motel has two swimming pools, which are open to non-residents, as well as other facilities and shops. It is an ideal place to come for a dip in the water, when sightseeing in hot weather is taking its toll. It is also relaxing because of the fine views and the relaxed atmosphere of the complex. Nearby is the motel disco, which is housed in a cave, and which plays mostly salsa and *merengue* dance music.

TRINIDAD EXCURSIONS

The main attractions outside Trinidad are the beautiful scenery of the Sierra del Escambray, which includes the Topes de Collantes, Valle de los Ingenios, and nearby beaches. These can either be visited by booking tours at a tourist desk (Cubatour, Rumbos or Cubancán are the main ones in Trinidad), or by taking a taxi, which will cost roughly the same as a tour if there are more than two of you.

Playa Ancón

About 10km (6.2 miles) south of Trinidad, this is the best beach resort in the area, with white sand and clean, turquoise water. The best part of the beach is in front of Hotel Ancón, which offers boat excursions for snorkelling and diving. It is a pleasant day trip from the town, but it should be mentioned that the beach is not quite up to the standard of those on the north coast.
10km (6 miles) south of Trinidad. Irregular bus services from Trinidad, although taxis and 'coco' taxis are always available in town to take you there for a few dollars.

Topes de Collantes

The most popular excursion from Trinidad takes you to the Parque Natural Topes de Collantes, offering lovely scenery in the unspoilt landscape of the Sierra del Escambray. There are several paths in the area offering stunning views of the lush forest and the opportunity to see wildlife such as butterflies, hummingbirds and even the *tocororo*, the national bird of Cuba, whose colours are reflected in the national flag.

At 800m (2,625ft) above sea level, and with good clean air, the area was the site of a sanitarium for lung diseases, and it is now an anti-stress centre and hotel.

The most popular trek takes you on a downward two-hour hike through the forest, passing curious rock formations, until you reach the Salto del Caburní, a steep, plunging waterfall that gushes

The Topes de Collantes

The Salto del Caburní waterfall

over rocks and collects in a lovely pool. Many people take their swimming costumes for a refreshing swim in the cool water; just the thing to prepare you for the steep climb back up!

A day tour by jeep is the most convenient way to visit the area, as the 30-minute drive north of Trinidad is steep and four-wheel drives are necessary to take you right to the start of the trek. A hire car or taxi will be unsuitable for the last part of the journey. Tours will often include a knowledgeable guide to describe the huge range of endemic species of flora and fauna, some with weird and wonderful features. Remember to wear strong shoes, as the walk is steep and rocky. Don't attempt the trek if it has been raining, as this makes the tracks slippery and highly dangerous.

SUGAR PLANTATIONS

Sugar has been the basis for Cuba's economy throughout its history. French sugar planters came to Cuba to escape the Haiti revolution, and brought their expertise with them. With the growing demand in Europe and America, large numbers of slaves needed to be imported from 1793 onwards to work in the sugar plantations and factories. Cuba became a plantation society, and was the biggest exporter of sugar in the world, with 1 million slaves accounting for more than half the population. This led to the emergence of sugar factories (*ingenios*), slave barracks (*barracones*), and religion, music and dance specific to the slave culture. For example, rumba music is thought to have developed from this culture.

Torre de Manaca Iznaga and Valle de los Ingenios

This valley is only 12km (7^1/$_2$ miles) from Trinidad, and is rich in history that reflects its importance as a producer of sugar in the 19th century. UNESCO has declared the valley a World Heritage Site as a result. The word *ingenios* means 'sugar mills'.

One way of seeing the valley is to take the steam train that leaves Trinidad daily and covers the entire valley. The railroad was built in 1919, because of its importance in transporting sugar cane. Cuba was in fact the first country in the Americas to build a railway. The railway takes one hour to reach the Manaca Iznaga Estate, where 350 slaves worked in the 1840s. The landowner's house now includes a restaurant and shops, but the main attraction is the tower, which gives impressive views over the surrounding countryside. It consists of seven levels, the first three square in shape, the top four octagonal, totalling a height of 45m (147ft). At the foot of the tower is the bell that tolled the work hours on the plantation and alerted the ranchers to an escaped slave.

Trains leave Trinidad at 9am and 1pm. It is best to check with the rail station first (Calle Bolívar 422; tel: 3348) or a tourist desk. The station is about 15 minutes' walk from the town centre. Please note that trains returning to Trinidad are irregular, which may mean that you are killing time at Manaca Iznaga waiting for the return train, once you have visited the tower. The alternative to the train is a taxi from the town centre which may be more convenient, especially if there are two or more of you.

Eastern Central Cuba

While Trinidad is the central attraction in the Eastern
Central provinces of Cuba, there is much else to do and
see, including excellent diving and swimming, and visits to
other colonial towns. The provinces here are Sancti
Spiritus, Ciego de Avila, Camagüey, Holguín and Las
Tunas: many have not seen much tourist development, but
the countryside is pretty, with swathes of sugar cane,
hillsides with thatched cottages, palm trees, and lovely bays
and beaches, protected by coral reefs. When he landed
here, Columbus himself stated that it was the most
beautiful country he had ever seen.

The sacred ceiba tree

It is easy to regard the towns in this area
simply as transit towns that break up the
journey between Havana, Trinidad and
Santiago de Cuba, but they have an
atmosphere of their own, vibrant and
authentically Cuban.

For example, Sancti Spiritus is an
attractive colonial town and was one of
the oldest towns on the island, being
founded in 1514. It receives few visitors
despite its status as a National
Monument. The capital of the province,
it suffers from its proximity to Trinidad,
its colonial charm not matching its
rival's well-preserved beauty.

Ciego de Avila on the other hand is a
more modern town, only becoming a
city in 1840. Also a provincial capital, it
has little of architectural interest, and
the visitors it has are mostly on their
way to the popular diving sites in the
Jardines Del Rey archipelago. The
province of Ciego de Avila is also
famous for activities such as freshwater
fishing and game shooting.

Las Tunas province, a small
agricultural province is often
forgotten by tourists. The capital is
an unpretentious and pleasant transit
town, but the main draws are the lovely
beaches. The province has 35 virgin
beaches, the most popular understandably
being Playa Covarrubias with a 3-km
(2-mile) coral reef and fine white sand.

CAMAGÜEY

The province of Camagüey is the largest
in the country, with flat but pretty
countryside. Its colonial capital city is
definitely not yet on the tourist map,
and it has a distinctly Cuban feel to
it, quite unlike the tourist towns of
Havana and Trinidad. However, much
restoration is being carried out on old
buildings and squares, and there is
much to see, particularly with regard to
the revolutionary history of the 19th
and 20th centuries. Saturday nights are
big nights in the town, with street
parties and a busy throng of Cubans,

young and old, enjoying the cool evening breeze in the squares and on the streets.

Camagüey is nicknamed 'the Legendary', on account of its traditions of heroism and patriotism. Several key figures are commemorated in the town, including Ignacio Agramonte, who was killed in action in 1873. Originally founded on the coast and gaining prosperity mainly through livestock and then sugar, the city was moved inland to escape pirate attacks.

CITY SIGHTS
Casa Natal de Ignacio Agramonte
The prestigious art collection in this museum is said to be second only to that in the Museo de Bellas Artes in Havana,

including works by the famous Cuban artist, Fidelio Ponce. This was the only military building in town, being the headquarters of the Spanish army cavalry in the 19th century. The museum was inaugurated in 1955 and includes exhibits on history, natural history, archaeology, and the art of the province.
Avenida de los Martires 2. Tel: 82425. Open: Tue–Sat 10am–6pm, Sun 8am–12pm. Admission charge.

Casa Natal de Ignacio Apramonte
This pretty two-storey house from 1750 was the former home of one of the national heroes in the struggle against Spanish colonialism. He was born in the house in 1841, becoming a lawyer

Eastern Central provinces

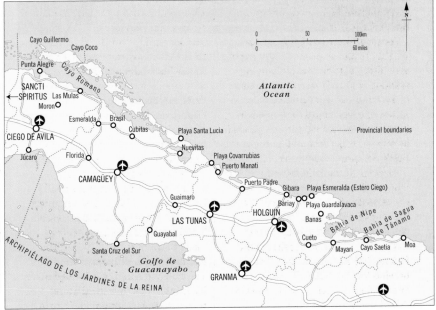

Statue of local hero, Ignacio Agramonte, in the square named after him

and cattle rancher before leading a rebellion in the area against the Spanish. He died in 1873 after being wounded in action. The top floor of the house is a museum displaying the patriot's personal belongings, while the beautiful courtyard is used for concerts. Note the old *tinajones* (clay jars) lying in the courtyard.
49 Avenida Ignacio Agramonte, opposite the church on Plaza de los Trabajadores. Tel: 297116. Open: Tue–Sat 10am–6pm, Sun 8am–12pm. Admission charge.

Catedral de Nuestra Señora de la Candelaria

The town's cathedral is on the south side of the park, and, along with the square itself, has undergone several restorations, including one in recent years. It is dedicated to Our Lady of Candelaria, the patron saint of the city. It was originally built in the early 18th century, but reconstructed in 1864, giving it its present-day appearance.
Calle Independencia 64, Parque Agramonte. Tel: 94965. Open: Mon 3.30–6pm, Tue–Sat 9.30–11.30am & 3.30–6pm.

Nuestra Señora de la Merced

The main attraction in this church is the Santo Sepulcro, a silver coffin, constructed in 1762 with the donation of 23,000 silver coins. Before the Revolution, it used to be carried in procession along the town streets.

The church was originally built in 1601, but rebuilt in 1756, resulting in a Baroque façade with a central bell tower. The interior has some striking murals that are almost Art Nouveau in style. A cemetery was on the original site of the church, and the catacombs can still be seen, including some bones and skulls. In the courtyard there are 19th-century cannons abandoned by the Spanish. The external clock on the church was the first public clock in the town. The church is slowly being restored.

Plaza de los Trabajadores 4. Tel: 92783. Open: Mon–Sat 3.30–6pm, Tue–Sat 9.30–11.30am & 3.30–6pm.

Parque Ignacio Agramonte
The main square in the town, this was initially the Plaza de Armas. It is a beautiful square with marble flooring, clean and very well restored. It is a hub for locals, especially in the evenings when residents of all ages come to sit around the square, enjoying the tranquil atmosphere and listening to musicians. The equestrian statue in the middle of the square is of a local independence hero, Ignacio Agramonte, who died in battle in 1873. Royal palms stand at the four corners of the

CAMAGÜEY'S PECULIARITIES

Despite the town being moved inland in the 17th century, it was still attacked by pirates, including the Welshman Henry Morgan. Architects began to design the town with narrow, irregular street networks, in order to confuse and deter attackers. It is a town layout that makes it very awkward to find your way around, so a good map is recommended.

Another peculiarity of Camagüey are the *tinajones*, which have become symbols of the city. These large jars are found everywhere, especially in the courtyards of colonial houses and in parks. They are made of clay from the nearby hills, and some can be as large as 2m (6½ft) in height. The jars were introduced by Catalonian immigrants in the early 1700s, and are still used today to collect rainwater and to store food.

square in memory of a group of nationalists executed here in 1851.

A *tinajon* clay jar

Cayo Coco

Although isolated from the rest of Cuba, Cayo Coco attracts a large number of tourists who stay here mostly on package holidays, but do not venture very far. For those interested in crystal-clear waters, fine white sand and warm water, Cayo Coco is idyllic, especially for families. The other attractions include some of the best ecotourist facilities in Cuba, with a natural reserve for marine birds, especially flamingoes.

The idyllic beach at Cayo Coco

Cayo Coco has become a focal point in the government's drive to develop Cuba as an ecotourist destination. Plans include a rapid expansion in large, luxury resorts, all built and operated by foreign businesses. The island of Cayo Coco, or the *coco*, as Cubans refer to it, is 374sq km (144 sq miles) in size, connected to the mainland just north of Morón by a 27-km (17-mile) causeway. It has 22km (14 miles) of sandy beaches, with the remaining land being partly marshy, abundant in mangroves and coconut palms.

Parador la Silla

The ideal spot for viewing flamingoes, which flock here between April and November (the wet season) to breed. It is a spectacle not to be missed.
On the end of the causeway furthest from the Cuban mainland.

Playa los Flamencos

Perhaps one of the best beaches on the island, Playa los Flamencos is renowned for its clear, shallow waters and white sand, extending for 5km (3 miles).

Flamingoes, after which the beach is named, can be seen all year round. There are now about 35,000 birds in the cays (islands), which have been encouraged to prosper here.
Near the northern tip of Cayo Coco island. 15 minutes' drive from hotels: most people take tours from the various hotels here.

Playa Prohibida

Anyone looking for peace and seclusion need look no further. This beach is appropriately named, since the government has banned construction here, in order to protect the environment. There is a nature trail which starts nearby and leads to the centre of Cayo Coco, and the beach itself is surrounded by large dunes, some rising as high as 40m (131ft).
Just a few miles west of the village of Güira.

CAYO GUILLERMO

This small island specialises in fishing, especially deep-sea fishing, and Ernest Hemingway was a dedicated fan of the area. The cay is protected by a long coral reef which is good for diving. The beach is 5km (3 miles) long, with some of the highest sand dunes in the area, covered in mangroves, palms and other trees such as mahogany and juniper.

On the northwest of Cayo Coco island, linked to it by a causeway.

The white sandy beach at Playa los Flamencos

Bahía de Bariay and Guardalavaca

While Bahía de Bariay and Guardalavaca are more than 30km (19 miles) apart, visitors to the area are unlikely to see one and not see the other. They are both highly recommended to tourists, but for different reasons. The first is a historically important site just off the colonial town of Gibara, while the latter is a mecca for sun-worshipping resort tourists.

View of the bay from Gibara Hill

Bahía de Bariay

Great views of this bay can be had by hiking up El Cuartelon (El Mirador). Most historians agree that Columbus landed here on October 28, 1492, on a spit of land in the middle of a bay (Cayo de Bariay), and was astounded by the beauty of the area. There is a monument here marking the 500th anniversary of his landing, called *Encuentro* (encounter), which is dedicated to the Taino Indians. The pretty town of Gibara has higgledy-piggledy deep-red tiled roofs; it was founded in 1817 and is still important for fishing.

Bahia de Bariay lies east of Gibara town, about 32km (20 miles) north of Holguín. The monument is relatively remote if travelling by car, but boat trips can be arranged from Guardalavaca.

Guardalavaca

The beach resort of Guardalavaca is the second most popular in Cuba, after Varadero, and is on a beautiful stretch of coastline, indented with horseshoe bays. It is famous for its lovely clear turquoise sea, fine sand and coral reefs close to the shore.

Although it is within easy reach of Holguín (58km or 36 miles), it still feels slightly isolated. The area has been extensively developed since the 1980s and is now a popular tourist resort. The name Guardalavaca literally means 'watch the cow', a Spanish term used for the cattle egret, a very common bird in this part of Cuba.

Guardalavaca Beach Resorts

There are two sections to the resort. The

COLUMBUS IN CUBA

Christopher Columbus recorded the occasion of his landing on Cuban soil for the first time, on October 28, 1492: 'Along the banks of the river were trees I have never seen at home, with flowers and fruit of the most diverse kinds, among the branches of which one heard the delightful chirping of birds... When I descended from the launch, I approached two fishermen's huts. Upon seeing me, the natives took fright and fled... This island is truly the most beautiful land human eyes have ever beheld.'

first is older, with a village feel to it, and is centred around Playa Guardalavaca. The crescent-shaped beach itself is 4km (2¹/₂ miles) long, enclosed at both ends by rocks, and backed by abundant vegetation. The second is a few kilometres west, around Playa Esmeralda. The newer, mostly all-inclusive resort hotels are here, with excellent facilities, although there is not much to do outside the hotel complex. Nevertheless, the beach (also known as Estero Ciego) is perfect for snorkelling.

Bahía de Naranjo

West of the beach is a natural park called Bahía de Naranjo, which is well known for its marina and aquarium. Sailing trips and sailing expeditions can be arranged from here, while the dolphin and sea lion shows at the aquarium are often included in tours of the area.

Chorro de Maita

For those with an interest in archaeology, this site is unmissable. It is the largest native Indian necropolis in Cuba and the Caribbean, where 56 Taino skeletons dating from 1490–1540 are preserved just as they were found. Although the museum is small, it is very well presented. A reconstruction of a pre-Columbian rural village is also here, with life-size statues of the natives.

Cerro de Yaguajay, Banes. Open: Mon–Fri 9am–5pm, Sun 9am–1pm.
Admission charge.

The beach at Guardalavaca

Holguín

The town of Holguín is a good base to explore some of the more interesting sights in the province of the same name, such as Bahía de Bariay where Columbus landed, and some of the best beaches in Cuba, particularly in Guardalavaca.

Plaza San José

The town itself is attractive and modern, with many leafy squares, hence its description as the 'city of parks'. Holguín was founded in 1545, and is named after García Holguín, a Spanish captain who helped colonise the area. Most of the architecture dates from the 19th and 20th centuries, and the streets have an air of pleasant tranquillity. It may have to do with the slow pace of the traffic, which is cluttered by hundreds of bicycles, the preferred form of transport for most residents.

The heart of the town is centred around Parque García (known commonly as Parque Central), with two parallel streets, Maceo and Libertad, forming the borders that contain the three main squares in the town: Parque Central, Parque Infantil and Parque Céspedes.

Plaza Central (Parque Calixto)

Many of the sights of interest in this town are around this square, including the Museo Provincial. It was named after General Calixto García Iñiguez, who captured the town from the Spanish in 1872 during the Wars of Independence, and his statue stands in the middle of the square. One block from the plaza is the building where he was born, Casa Natal de Calixto García.

The square really comes to life at night when families and friends congregate to enjoy the cool air, and listen to the music coming from nearby bars, especially the excellent Casa de la Trova.

Lomo de la Cruz

Called 'Hill of the Cross', there are marvellous views from the top, a feature that was utilised by the town engineers. A cross was placed here on May 3, 1790 by a Franciscan priest, but it was blown down in 1998 by Hurricane Georges. Every May 3, locals commemorate the occasion, called *Romerías de la Cruz de Mayo*. There is also a lookout tower built by the Spanish, 127m (417ft) above the town.
The hill is 3km (2 miles) northwest of Parque Central and may be ascended on foot (up 458 steps) or by road.

Museo de Historia Natural

This is one of the most interesting natural history museums in Cuba, with an impressive collection of birds and shells. There are 11 rooms with 7,000 specimens, including a 60-million-year-old fossilised fish. The museum contains many stuffed animals, including a manatee and giant turtle, and the building is also attractive, with neoclassical pillars and Moorish turrets.

Calle Maceo 129, between Martí and Luz Caballero. Just off Parque Central. Open: Tue–Sat 9am–10pm, Sun 9am–9pm. Admission charge.

Museo Provincial ('La Periquera')

The name 'parrot cage' for this museum comes from the brightly coloured soldiers who guarded the barracks in the 19th century, who came to be known as *periquitos* (parakeets). The museum illustrates the history of Holguín, including its important role in the wars of independence, which liberated the city from the Spanish in 1872. Also exhibited are archaeological relics of the Taíno Indians from the 8th to the 15th centuries. The most famous item is a carved stone axe head, the *Hacha de Holguín*, now the symbol of the city.

Calle Frexes 198, between Manduley and Maceo. Overlooks Plaza Central. Tel: 463395. Open: Mon–Fri 8am–9pm, Sat 9am–5pm. Admission charge.

View of the city from the steps of La Loma de la Cruz

Santiago de Cuba

Santiago de Cuba is a wholly different proposition to Havana or indeed to any other Cuban city. Its position on the east coast of the island has given it a very Caribbean flavour in terms of climate, people and culture. As the second city in Cuba after Havana, it is of great importance to the traveller in understanding the country, its culture and history.

Moncada Barracks

The city is protected from sea breezes, and sits in a bay surrounded by mountains, making it several degrees warmer than Havana. It is more musical, more passionate and livelier than the rest of the island, and is most famous for its Carnival each July, an experience full of colour, energy and raucous celebration. Some travellers notice the more brazen nature of locals approaching foreigners in the street, offering accommodation, a meal, or transport among other things. Do not come expecting beautiful colonial architecture, wide avenues and tranquil streets. However, the residents are friendly, lively and love to dance the night away. Once you get used to the rhythm of the city and the nature of the locals, you will enjoy Santiago de Cuba.

Indomitable character

The city is known as the 'Cradle of the Revolution'. It was in Santiago that Fidel

A colourful mural on Calle Heredia

Castro launched the struggle against dictator Batista by attacking the Moncada barracks, and it was in the nearby mountains of the Sierra Maestra that Castro and Che Guevara planned their guerilla warfare that was to lead to the triumph of the Cuban Revolution. One hundred years earlier, local nationalists led the wars of independence against the Spanish.

The city is one of the oldest in the country, with many sites of historical and cultural interest, as well as many excursions to take you away from the traffic and fumes of the city, with visits to stunning beaches and scenic landscapes.

Architecture and culture
The city centre itself feels cluttered, with more energy and noise than other Cuban towns, but with buildings in much better condition than in Havana. It certainly does not have the colonial beauty of Trinidad, but it has an eclectic mix of architectural styles and colour.

The people and music have a distinctly Afro-Caribbean emphasis, with the religion *santeria* playing an important role in many people's lives. The music is influenced by the large numbers of immigrants that came here from French colonies, particularly Haiti, and the music and dancing are certainly more energetic, especially noticeable at carnival time.

Santiago de Cuba town centre

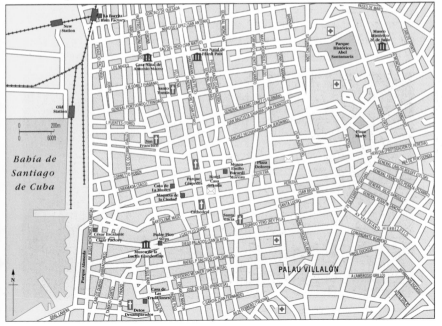

AROUND PARQUE CÉSPEDES

Parque Céspedes is the heart of the town, with many of the sights and museums within easy walking distance. Formerly the Plaza de Armas, it was renamed Parque Céspedes in honour of the nation's founding father, whose statue stands in the middle. It is very well maintained and policed, in an attempt to make the square as attractive to tourists as possible. Neoclassical in style, the square is flanked on the east side by the luxurious Hotel Casa Granda. Calle Heredia, which runs along one side of the square, is the most famous and lively street in the town, especially at night, when music venues such as the Casa de la Trova kick into action.

Parque Céspedes flanked by Hotel Casa Granda and the Cathedral

The dining room in the Museo de Ambiente Cubano

Casa Natal de José María Heredia

This is a more modest house than that of Diego Velázquez (*see p118*), but it has an understated elegance. A national monument, it is the birthplace of the famous Cuban poet, José María Heredia, who is credited with transforming Latin

Bedroom in the Museo de Ambiente Cubano

American poetry. He was exiled at the age of 20 for his involvement in an independence conspiracy and wrote his most famous ode to nature, *Niagra*, in the USA before his tragic death at the age of 36. This 18th-century house is very well preserved, and contains period wooden ceilings, tiled floors and furniture. The courtyard is pretty, with wooden columns, vegetation and a stone well. The building is also used as a cultural centre, with weekly poetry workshops.

Heredia 260, between Hartmann and Pío Rosado (Carniceria). Open: Tue–Sat 9am–8pm, Sun 9am–1pm. Admission charge.

Catedral de Nuestra Señora de la Asunción

The cathedral of Santiago has had a troubled history, needing to be rebuilt

four times, on account of a combination of earthquakes, pirate attacks and other disasters. This national monument stands out among the beautiful buildings around Parque Céspedes, and its most recent restoration has been a great success. The original building dates from 1524, with the most recent changes being made in 1922. As a result, there are a number of styles on display.
Calle Heredia, on the south side of Parque Céspedes. Tel: 628502. Open: Tue–Fri 8am–12pm & 5–6.30pm, Sat 8am–12pm & 4–5pm. Services Tue–Fri 6.30pm, Sat 5pm, Sun 9am & 6.30pm.

Hotel Casa Granda

There are many points of interest at this hotel, which is one of the most elegant buildings in Santiago. Opened in 1914, it was patronised by many stars of the time, including Babe Ruth and Joe Louis. Graham Greene described it in his famous novel *Our Man in Havana* as a hotel frequented by spies. Now it is the perfect place to have a drink or snack from the terrace bar and café, and watch the activity in Parque Céspedes, or to enjoy the views over the city from the fifth floor. It is also a useful place for internet access, while the offices under the hotel offer tourist and exchange services (the Asistur office is the only place in Cuba that accepts American Express travellers' cheques).
Heredia 201, on the east side of Parque Céspedes. Tel: 686600. Charge for going up to the fifth floor bar 8pm–1am, but this buys you your first cocktail.

Museo de Ambiente Cubano

Perhaps the best museum in the town,

SANTIAGO'S CARNIVAL

Carnival in Santiago is based on many African and Franco-Haitian elements, most of them religious. Festivities have been held between June 24 and July 26 in Santiago since the end of the 17th century, with the aim of honouring the city's patron saint, Santiago Apostolo. In the 17th century, slaves were allowed into the streets after the processions to sing, dance and play music. These were the forerunners of the Carnival groups, or *comparsas*, who wear masks or costumes, and carry streamers and banners and brightly coloured paper lamps (*farolas*). The chief dance is the *conga*, where people form a procession and dance through the streets. The whole town erupts into a frenzy of celebration and partying during the second half of July, a truly memorable experience.

and certainly the one with most character, is the Museo de Ambiente Cubano. It is the oldest private home in Cuba, and is full of furniture, china, porcelain and other objects. One really gets a feel for how the residents lived at the time. It was built around 1530 as a residence for Governor Diego Velázquez, who conquered Cuba. He lived on the top floor, while the ground floor, which was used to smelt gold, was called the 'House of Transactions'. One can still see the old furnace where the gold ingots were made. Each room shows a particular period of history, including Creole furniture from the 16th century, 19th-century furniture heavily influenced by the French style, and 19th-century stained-glass windows.

A guided tour is recommended.
Calle Felix Peña 612, on the northwest corner of Parque Céspedes. Tel: 652652. Open: Sept–Apr daily 9am–4.45pm; May–Aug Mon–Fri 9am–5.45pm, Sat 9am–5pm, Sun 9am–12.45pm. Admission charge, plus charges for tours and taking photos.

Museo del Carnaval

If you are not able to attend the Santiago Carnival in July, this is the next best thing. Among the exhibits are musical instruments, papier-mâché masks, banners and costumes, all of which give a flavour of this most famous of festivities. The courtyard of this lovely 18th-century building is used for folk events and concerts, as well as rehearsals by performers at the Carnival.
Calle Heredia 303, corner of Pío Rosado (Carniceria). Tel: 626955. Open: Tue–Sat 9am–8pm, Sun 9am–5pm. Admission charge.

Museo Emilio Bacardí Moreau

The oldest and perhaps the most eclectic museum in Cuba houses mementoes of the Wars of Independence, mummies from Egypt and South America, and both colonial and modern Cuban paintings. A tour is recommended.

The museum was named after the main benefactor, the industrialist and founder of the famous rum distillery, Emilio Bacardí Moreau. He was the first mayor of Cuba when it became a republic. The museum was founded in 1828, and the building was purpose-built in the neoclassical style.
Calle Pío Rosada (Carniceria), corner of Aguilera, two blocks east of the Parque Central. Tel: 628402. Open: Tue–Sat 9.15am–8.15pm, Sun 9am–12.15pm, Mon 2–8.15pm. Admission charge.

Carnival fervour in Santiago

Walk: Parque Céspedes, Santiago de Cuba

This area in the centre of Santiago is the most pleasant in the town, with well-restored buildings and lots of sights of historical and cultural interest.

Allow 4 hours.

The walk starts in Parque Céspedes. The streets in this area are often busy, with constant movement from vehicles of every description as well as people. It is easy to get involved in a conversation with locals interested in offering you some kind of service, and it is best to be easy-going but firm. Remember not to rush around, as the heat can be exhausting for the uninitiated. Distances are small, making it easy to escape to the cool of the Hotel Casa Granda for a rest and a drink.

1 Museo de Ambiente Cubano

The home of the Spanish conquistador Diego Velázquez has been lovingly preserved, and is one of the most fascinating museums in Cuba. Remember to get a guide, as there is little written explanation of the exhibits.

Turn left on Félix Peña and right on Aguilera.

2 Ayuntamiento (Casa del Gobierno)

Although this white Moorish building is not open to the public, it is of interest because of its historical importance. It was here on January 1, 1959 that Fidel Castro made his first speech to the Cuban people on the day that dictator Batista fled the country and the Cuban

Revolution triumphed. This building was built in 1950 to 18th-century designs and is now used as the town hall for local government.

Facing the square, turn left and walk eastwards along Aguilera for two blocks, until you reach a white neoclassical building on your right.

3 Museo Emilio Bacardí Moreau

This houses an eclectic range of exhibits, from historical artefacts, colonial paintings, modern art and archaeology. A guided tour is recommended in order to make the most of the museum.

Walking down the steps of the museum, turn left then right onto Calle Heredia, perhaps the most well-known street in the town, looking at the buildings on your left.

4 Casa Natal de José María Heredia

This modest but elegant museum was the birthplace of the famous Cuban poet, José Heredia, with some beautiful furniture and antique lamps. The shaded courtyard will give you a welcome break from the heat.

Continue walking west along Calle Heredia, crossing Hartmann and looking left.

5 Casa de la Trova

This famous music venue is one of the

most popular in town for live Cuban music. More touristy than other music venues, it still retains its vibrancy and character, especially at night.
Looking towards Parque Céspedes, cross Lacret.

6 Catedral de Nuestra Señora de la Asunción

The cathedral of Santiago is very well preserved, although it has been rebuilt several times. The façade is neoclassical while the original church was built four centuries ago. Some say that Diego Velázquez is buried beneath the building.

Continue walking westwards along Heredia and turn left when you reach Corona. Look right when you reach the corner of this block.

7 Balcón de Velázquez

This spacious terrace offers a grand view of the port and bay of Santiago, as well as the picturesque quarter of Tivolí. It was built on the site of a Spanish fortress. There is an admission charge here, but the views are well worth it. One can also buy drinks and sit in the shade to recover from the exertions of the walk.

Walk around Parque Céspedes

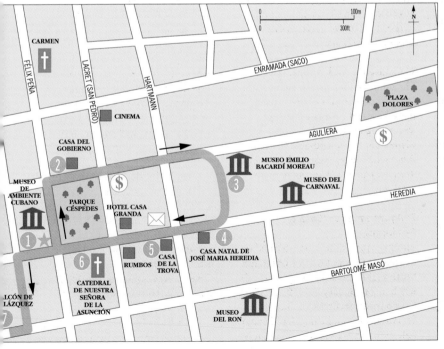

Beyond the city centre

Venturing out of the heart of the city is well recommended, as there are several interesting sites of historical importance, particularly the Moncada Barracks. Some are only a short walk from Parque Céspedes, such as the Padre Pico steps and the Museo de Lucha Clandestina.

The Moncada Barracks, now a museum and school

Calle Saco

This important street (also called 'Enramada') links the old city with the port and is Santiago's main commercial street. The area nearest Parque Céspedes is a working-class quarter with some interesting early 20th-century wooden houses. At the bottom of the sloping street is the Paseo Mar(i)timo, which retains the original paving from the 1840s, although it has lost its former elegance as the seafront promenade for the colonial city's high society. The promenade stretches out along the port.

Casa Natal de Antonio Maceo

One of the great generals in the Wars of Independence was born in this modest house in 1845. Maceo rejected the peace agreement in 1878 that ended the Ten Years War against the Spanish, and after a period in exile, returned to liberate the island in the final and decisive War of Independence by 1898. The museum houses his personal belongings, including family photographs.
207 Los Maceo, between Calles Corona and Rastro. Tel: 623750. Open Mon–Sat 9am–5pm. Admission charge.

THE ATTACK ON THE MONCADA BARRACKS

The attack on the Moncada Barracks on July 26, 1953 marked a turning point in the revolutionary struggle from peaceful means to armed conflict. The aim of the attack was to capture the barracks with its huge arsenal of weapons, and take control of the neighbourhood, which included a hospital and law courts. Using popular support in the area, they hoped that their revolution would quickly spread beyond the city. With a force of 100-odd rebels, Castro used the noisy Carnival celebrations as the perfect time to launch the daring raid. The attack failed mainly because they ran into an army patrol, and the ensuing gunfight raised the 800-strong garrison from their sleep. Hopelessly outnumbered, eight of the rebels were killed and 55 were taken prisoner, tortured and executed. Fidel Castro and many others were captured in the nearby mountains but their lives were saved by the capturing army officer who recognised Castro from their university days. Castro was to resume the revolutionary struggle after his period in prison and exile when he landed in Cuba in December 1956 on the yacht *Granma*.

Cementerio de Santa Ifigenia

This is a grand and well-kept cemetery which is the second most important on the island after the Colón cemetery in Havana. It contains graves, tombs and monuments of some of Cuba's patriotic heroes, most notable of which is José Martí's mausoleum. This large octagonal structure is surrounded by six statues of women, representing the six Cuban provinces in the 19th century. The statue of Martí inside is designed to receive a shaft of light all morning. Other tombs include those of Carlos Manuel de Céspedes, Emilio Bacardí, and Tomás Estrada Palma, who was the first president of Cuba. It is said that Fidel Castro will be buried here.

Avenida Crombet, Reparto Juan G Gómez, in the northwest of the city. Tel: 632723. Open: daily 7am–6pm. Charge for admission and photos. Includes guided tour.

Cuartel Moncada (Museo Histórico 26 de Julio)

One of the most important days in Cuba's history happened here in the Moncada Barracks, now a school and home to the Museo Histórico 26 de Julio. This was the site of the failed attack by Fidel Castro's revolutionaries on the second largest garrison in Cuba on July 26, 1953. This led to the capture and execution of many of the revolutionaries, and the imprisonment and exile of others, including Fidel Castro.

The bullet holes from the attack have been left on the building walls, while there is a detailed and fascinating exhibit on the events of the day, as well as the Cuban revolutionary struggle of the late 1950s. It includes blood-stained uniforms from that fateful day as well as possessions of the revolutionaries used in the revolutionary struggle. A guided tour is recommended as the exhibits are in spanish.

Calle General Portuondo (Trinidad), between Moncada and Avenida de los Libertadores. Tel: 620157. Open: Tue–Sat 9am–7.30pm, Sun 9am–1pm. Admission charge includes guided tour. No photos allowed.

Museo Abel Santamaría

For those interested in the Cuban Revolution, this museum is also worth visiting. It is part of the Parque Histórico Abel Santamaría, which also includes the Moncada Barracks, Saturnino Lora hospital and the law court buildings.

In the 1953 raid on the Moncada Barracks, a group of men led by Abel Santamaría targeted the Saturnino hospital, a strategic site on a hill overlooking the barracks. They were captured, tortured and killed, with Santamaría having his eyes gouged out. Now all Cuban eye hospitals bear his name.

This museum focuses primarily on the trial of Fidel Castro and his men, held a few days after the attack. Castro's landmark self-defence speech manuscript is housed here, the now legendary 'History Will Absolve Me' speech. There are also photos showing the great hardship, socially and economically, that Cuba underwent during the 1950s.

Calle General Portuondo, corner of Avenida de los Libertadores. Tel: 624119. Open: Mon–Sat 9am–5pm. Admission charge.

The famous Padre Pico steps in the Tivoli area

Museo de la Lucha Clandestina

One of the most beautiful colonial buildings in the city (Loma del Intendente), this yellow building houses the Museum of the Clandestine Struggle, giving an interesting account of the activities of the Movimiento 26 de Julio, the underground struggle against Batista's dictatorship. The building, which was originally the headquarters of Batista's police, was a prime target for the revolutionaries, and was burnt down in 1956. The exhibits revolve around Frank País, the leader of the movement, who led a revolt in Santiago that tried to coincide with the landing of Fidel Castro's revolutionaries in Cuba in December 1956. The revolt was repressed and País was assassinated by Batista's police the following year.

Frank País' funeral was massively attended by Santiagueros, a signal that the Revolution would have significant local support. Other photos document the years of tension and conflict which led up to the rebels' triumph.

Calle Jesus Rabí 1, between Santa Rita and San Carlos, at the top of the Padre Pico steps. Tel: 624689. Open: Tue–Sat 9am–7pm, Sun 9am–5pm. Admission charge. Guide recommended, as the exhibits are in Spanish.

Padre Pico steps

These steps leading up to the Tivoli area of the city are famous partly because the opening shots in Fidel Castro's first offensive against Batista were fired from here. The steps were named after Bernardo del Pico, a priest who helped the poor in Santiago, and built by Emilio Bacardí, the mayor at the time and founder of the famous rum factory. The steps lead to the most colourful neighbourhood in the city, populated in the late 1700s by newly arrived French immigrants who were escaping the revolution in Haiti. The Tivoli area was named after the theatre built there.

One of the most original and best music venues in the city is in this area, the Casa de las Tradiciones on Jesus Rabí, a few blocks south from the Museo de Lucha Clandestina. Today the steps are home to domino and chess players, who sit all day enjoying a quiet game.

Near the bottom of Castillo Duany. The steps lead up to the Museo de Lucha Clandestina and Calle Padre Pico.

Plaza de la Revolución

This rather soulless square is dominated by a huge and impressive monument, showing General Antonio Maceo, the 19th-century revolutionary, on horseback, surrounded by stylised representations of machetes. The monument is distinctly Soviet in style, being constructed in the early 1990s by Alberto Lezcay, a local sculptor.

It is in this square that major speeches and rallies are held, including the mass said by Pope John Paul II during his visit in 1998.

In the block where Avenida de las Américas meets Avenida de los Libertadores (Carretera Central).

Excursions from Santiago de Cuba

A wide range of excursions is possible from Santiago. Some are available as day trips using one of the many tour agencies, while for some you may need to organise your own transport. The Rumbos office opposite Hotel Casa Granda is perhaps the most used, although many of the big hotels outside of the city centre also have tourist desks where one can book tours. Overall, they are excellent value, enabling you to visit several sights in one day, often with lunch included.

View from the Gran Piedra

Castillo del Morro

A hugely interesting and picturesque sight is the historic Castillo del Morro, an imposing cliff-top fort at the entrance to the bay of Santiago. It has been declared a UNESCO World Heritage Site, and has been relatively well maintained, even though it is nearly 370 years old. It was built by Giovan Battista Antonelli upon the order of the governor of the time, Pedro de la Roca, as a much-needed defence against pirates and corsairs (mercenary ships commissioned by enemy countries).

The ramparts of Castillo del Morro

The sanctuary of El Cobre

There are many rooms worth visiting, including the munitions room, prison cells, chapel, and rooms where torture was practised. The bay was the scene of the decisive naval battle in which the US fleet attacked the city and defeated the Spanish fleet, which led to the independence of Cuba. Every evening at sunset, there is the ceremonial firing of a cannon.

Carretera del Morro, 10km (6 miles) southwest of Santiago. Tel: 691569. Open: daily 8am–7pm. Admission charge, plus charge for the use of a camera.

Cayo Granma

Often included in tours to the Castillo del Morro, this is home to a picturesque little fishing island, made up of multicoloured huts and small houses, some of which are on stilts in the water.

It only takes about 30 minutes to walk around the island, and is a good way to see the locals' way of life in a relaxing environment. There are no vehicles, which makes it an enjoyable place to stroll. Cayo Granma was originally named Cayo Smith, after its wealthy owner, and it was at one time a resort for the rich.

Cayo Granma can be accessed by ferry from Marina Punta, 8km (5 miles) southwest of Santiago, at the end of Carretera Turistica.

'El Cobre'

An attractive church in a picture-book setting, El Sanctuario de Nuestra Señora de la Caridad del Cobre (El Cobre) is the most famous church in Cuba. It contains the shrine of Cuba's patron saint, the Virgen de la Caridad del

Cobre, a wooden statue of a black Madonna.

Nowadays there are pilgrimages to this basilica from all over the country, and many mementoes are donated in gratitude, some of which are displayed. They include Ernest Hemingway's Nobel Prize medal, cups and medals from Cuban sports heroes, and earth collected by Cuban soldiers who fought in Angola. The statue of the Virgin is richly dressed with gold and jewels, and kept in an air-conditioned box, which revolves to face the basilica for Mass. Nearby is a copper (*cobre*) mine, which was worked by hundreds of slaves until 1807.

Village of El Cobre, 10km (6 miles) west of Santiago, off Carretera Central 21. Tel: 36131. Open: daily 8am–6pm. There is an annual procession here on September 8. Women with exposed shoulders are not admitted, although coveralls can be hired if necessary. There are many touts selling flowers and candles for offering at the church, as well as

Colonial building at the Isabelica coffee plantation

LA VIRGEN DEL COBRE

Legend has it that in 1606 three fishermen in the Bay of Nipe were about to capsize when they found the statue of the Virgin nailed to a plank of wood, floating in the sea. They were saved and brought the statue to the church, where it soon became an object of veneration for locals, even non-Catholics, who attributed miraculous powers to it. The mixture of African cult beliefs brought by the slaves and Spanish Catholicism has developed a range of corresponding saints and gods. For example, the Virgin is associated with the Afro-Cuban goddess Ochún, who is always depicted as a beautiful black woman wearing yellow.

youths pestering you to buy bits of copper rock for a few cents.

Gran Piedra

This is one of the area's most popular excursions, the main draw being the spectacular view from the top of this giant rock, which rests on the crater of an extinct volcano. Well over 1,000m (3,250ft) tall, and weighing 75,000 tonnes (73,820 long tons), it can be reached by climbing the 450-odd steps from the road. The drive here takes you around hairpin bends and into cooler temperatures as you ascend. It is worth the journey, as the view of the lush countryside is one of the best in Cuba. Some say that one can see Haiti and Jamaica on a clear day, and their lights at night.

Jardín Botánico, 26km (16 miles) east of Santiago. Open: daily. Small charge to climb the rock, but free if on a day tour.

Granjita Siboney

Another important historical site linked to the Cuban Revolution is this farmhouse, used as the headquarters and base in the run-up to the assault on the Moncada Barracks. It is now a museum containing uniforms, weapons and artefacts, as well as newspaper accounts of the attacks. It was rented in 1953 by Abel Santamaría, the only revolutionary originally from Santiago. It is said that many of the bodies of the executed revolutionaries from the attack on the barracks were taken here and guns placed by their bodies to make it look as though Batista's men had killed them in a gun battle at the farmhouse.
Carretera de la Gran Piedra, 16km (10 miles) east of Santiago. Tel: 639168. Open: Tue–Sat 9am–5pm. Admission charge.

THE ORIGINS OF COFFEE GROWING IN CUBA

French coffee growers in Haiti were forced to flee that country in 1791 on account of the revolution there, and the nearest island was Cuba. By this time, coffee was already a popular drink among the European bourgeoisie. Soon, the hills around Santiago and the area between Guantánamo and Baracoa were full of coffee trees. The land here was ideal as it offered both shade and water, and the demand for coffee was such that by 1820 there were 191 plantations, and around 42,000 imported slaves. French growers made their fortunes and built impressive manor houses on their plantations.

Museo Isabelica

One of numerous old coffee plantations around the Gran Piedra, but the best maintained, is this museum, once the home of French landowners from Haiti. It is a fascinating museum which gives an authentic impression of life on a 19th-century coffee plantation. The downstairs was used by labourers and for the storage of tools, while the upstairs was the living quarters of the owners. The plantation was named after Isabel María, the lover and house-slave of the owner, Victor Constantin. When slavery was ended, he fled and – according to legend, at least – Isabel was thrown by the former slaves into a burning oven.
Carretera de la Gran Piedra 14km (9 miles) east of Santiago. It is within walking distance of Gran Piedra via a path from the foot of the rock. Open: daily 8am–4pm. Admission charge.

Valle de la Prehistoria

One of the most original amusement parks in the country is this huge children's park which includes a Natural History Museum. It is divided into logical areas according to evolutionary periods and features life-size models of dinosaurs and Stone Age men. It is well worth engaging an English-speaking guide to give a fascinating explanation of the prehistoric animals and their evolution. Remember to take a hat and lots of water, as it can get very hot walking around in the scorching sun, and there is little shade.
Carretera Baconaois 6.5km. Tel: 639239. Open: daily 8am–4.45pm. Admission charge.

Driving tour: eastern environs of Santiago

The east of Santiago is full of places to visit, from historical locations and children's attractions, to places in which to enjoy nature at its best. The area is known as Parque Baconao, and has been declared a biosphere reserve by UNESCO, having been developed mainly in the 1980s.
Allow a whole day.

The tour starts in Santiago de Cuba and takes you along the main sights east of the city. You can choose to stop the tour at Valle de la Prehistoria, or continue on for another 25km (16 miles) or so to the final sight on the tour, the aquarium. The road going east out of the city is the Carretera Siboney which takes you along the coast.

The road passes Abel Santamaría and Sevilla and divides at a village called Las Guásimas. Take the left-hand road, signposted to Gran Piedra. This steep road winds its way for 12km (7¹/₂ miles) up the hillside. Tour buses often stop for passengers to admire the coffee trees on the roadside and souvenir stalls.

1 Gran Piedra

This enormous monolith is at an altitude of 1,230m (4,035ft), with spectacular views of the surrounding tropical and mountain forests. You may not be able to see Haiti and Jamaica, but the view is certainly worth climbing the 450-odd steps from the bottom.
Drive back down for 2km (1 mile), until you reach 'Jardines de la Siberia'. Turn left.

2 Cafetal Isabelica

This is one of the few former coffee plantations in the area not in ruins, and it was once owned by French émigrés from Haiti. The buildings now house a museum, and you can see a demonstration of how coffee is grown and processed.
Continue down the road towards Las Guásimas, and turn left there to get back onto the Carretera Siboney. Drive for a couple of kilometres, looking out for a white and red farmhouse on the right.

3 La Granjita Siboney

This historical site is important because it was the base of operations for young revolutionaries in 1953, from which they launched their attack on the Moncada Barracks. The building is now a museum with uniforms and other memorabilia from the time. There are stone tributes on the side of the road around the area commemorating the spots where some of the revolutionaries were killed after the Moncada Barracks attacks.
Continue along the Carretera Siboney and take the right-hand road at La Estrella, going southwards to Siboney.

4 Playa Siboney

An ideal stop for a rest and lunch, this is the nearest beach to Santiago. There are several *paladar* restaurants and food stalls here. The beach is pleasant, and with a reef just offshore it is excellent for snorkelling.

Drive back to La Estrella and turn right to get back on the main provincial road heading east (Carretera Baconaois). You will pass El Oasis and Damajayabo.

5 Valle de la Prehistoria

This huge children's park is worth stopping at for an hour or two, as it offers a fascinating insight into the prehistoric world. Fans of the *Jurassic Park* films will find it especially interesting. Remember to take lots of water and a hat, as it can get very hot here in the middle of the day.

The final stop is 25km (16 miles) away going eastwards along the coast, past El Cupey and El Verraco, on the road to Baconao.

6 Acuario Banconao

The aquarium and dolphinarium here are popular with children and adults alike. There are three dolphin and sea-lion shows per day, as well as excellent displays of turtles, sharks and other species of fish, which can be seen at close range from a subterranean tunnel. Visitors can swim with the dolphins for an extra fee.

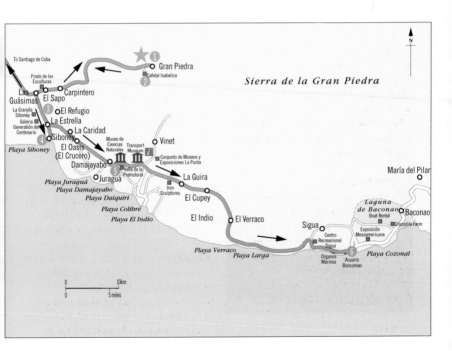

The rest of Eastern Cuba

Many visitors to the East of Cuba do not venture further than Santiago de Cuba, which is a shame considering the wealth of attractions that the area has to offer. There are several distinct areas, each of which has its own identity, and the provinces here are Granma, Santiago de Cuba and Guantánamo.

Bust of Chief Hatuey, Baracoa

The majestic Sierra Maestra mountains to the west are strongly associated with the guerilla war in the 1950s. Fidel Castro and the other revolutionaries landed in the southwest corner of the island before establishing guerilla bases in the mountains nearby. The south coast has some beautiful beaches, while the road between Manzanillo and Cabo Cruz has some of the most wild and spectacular scenery in the country.

The area around Santiago de Cuba is clad in pine forests and coffee plantations, while the Sierra Maestra mountains dominate the area, reaching almost to the sea.

Even more mountainous is the east of the island and the province of Guantánamo. Visitors will know the area mainly for the US naval base here, but there are other more interesting sights in the province. The area has a more Caribbean and French feel to it, being influenced by immigrants from the former French colony of Haiti, which is only 80km (50 miles) from Cuba's most easterly point. The coastal town of Baracoa is growing in popularity, not only because of its beautiful location on the tropical coast, but also because of its distinctive atmosphere and nightlife which attracts more intrepid travellers.

BARACOA

Although it is relatively isolated from the main tourist trails, Baracoa is gaining popularity, especially with independent travellers who are attracted by its laid-back atmosphere, friendly

Forest around the Sagua-Baracoa mountain range

people and lovely beaches. The Cubans have a saying, 'Baracoa means nature', which rings true, but the true origin of the name is from the Amerindian language, meaning 'existence of the sea'.

The area is a UNESCO biosphere reserve, with ten rivers, including the widest river in Cuba, the Río Toa. Baracoa provides 80 per cent of the country's coconut, while there are many beautiful waterfalls and 120 different types of tree. It is also the wettest region in Cuba.

Although just a small town, Baracoa's size belies its importance, since it is the oldest city in Cuba, discovered by Christopher Columbus in 1492. The architecture is certainly not colonial, but is instead a mixture of styles, with much French influence. Luxurious vegetation is everywhere, and in fact seems to invade the town itself, some wooden buildings being virtually overcome by nature.

The town was founded in 1512 by Diego Velázquez and called Nuestra Señora de la Asunción de Baracoa. It was the capital of Cuba for three years, before Velázquez transferred his residence to Santiago. This marked the beginning of a long period of isolation for the town, which has enabled the residents to maintain traditions and to preserve the environment. Through the centuries the town has supported itself by cultivating cocoa, coconuts and

The Eastern tip of Cuba

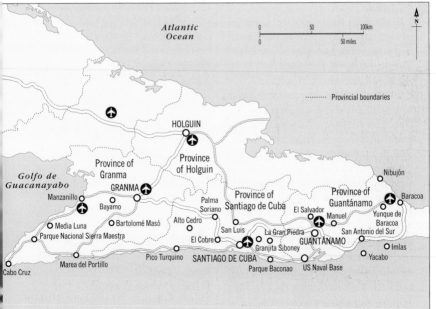

bananas, and by fishing. The town's isolation decreased in the 1960s with the building of the viaduct, La Farola, which has created one of the most spectacular roads on the island.

Baracoa is small and compact, and there are not many sights of any major significance, but a very pleasant walk can be had in the streets of the town centre.

Castillo de Seboruco

The view from the terrace of this 18th-century fortress is the best in town, looking over the roofs to the bay. It sits on a hill above the town and is now the Hotel El Castillo.
Calle Calixto García. Tel: 42103.

Catedral de Nuestra Señora de la Asunción

This church is most famous as the home of the Cruz de la Parra, a wooden cross that is said to be the oldest symbol of Christianity in the New World. According to legend, Christopher Columbus brought the cross on his first voyage to America, placing it on December 1, 1492 on the spot where Baracoa was later founded. This modest church was built in 1512, burnt down by the French, and rebuilt in 1805.
Calle Maceo 152. Tel: 43352. Open: Tue–Fri 8am–12pm, 2–5pm, Sat 8am–12pm, Sun mass at 9am.

El Malecón

The ideal time to stroll along the seafront is during the week when it is quieter, as the road houses the bustling food market on Saturday mornings, while the *noche baracoesa*, a lively folk festival, is held here on Saturday nights. *El Malecón runs across the whole of the north seafront of the town, between Fuerte Matachí in the east and Fuerte de la Punta on the western tip.*

Hotel La Rusa

Halfway along the Malecon is this historic hotel, named after its original owner, Magdalena Rovieskuya, of aristocratic background, who left Russia in 1917 and ended up in Baracoa, building this hotel. She was affectionately known in the area as 'Mima', and she supported the Revolution with funds, entertaining Castro and Che at her hotel during the revolutionary struggle. She was later immortalised in the book *The Consecration of Spring* by Alejo Carpentier. The hotel has interesting photos and relics in the foyer.
Máximo Gómez 13. Tel: 43011.

Museo Municipal (Fuerte Matachín)

An interesting overview of local history is given in this small museum, housed in a colonial fortress built as a defence against pirates. The museum has an impressive natural history section, including *Polymita* snails which are famous in the town. Another highlight is the only armaments magazine of its type in Cuba, dating from 1739.
Calle Martí y Malecón. Tel: 42122. Open: daily 8am–12pm, 2–6pm. Admission charge.

Parque Central (Parque Independencia)

The bust of the Indian leader Hatuey is located within this square, overlooked by the cathedral. The area comes to life in the evenings when residents young and old congregate here, although in the daytime there are many snack stalls selling good sandwiches and drinks. The Casa de la Trova and tourist information office are all close by.

Excursions from Baracoa

There are some notable trips from the town which are worth mentioning. Playa Maguana is a lovely beach 22km (13 miles) from Baracoa, with white sand. The most spectacular of Baracoa's rivers is the Río Yumurí, 30km (18 miles) east of the town. You can take an organised trip here to visit a *cacao* farm and to fish. Another worthwhile trip is to the top of *El Yunque* to view the breathtaking scenery from 575m (1,870ft) above sea level.

View of Baracoa Bay from Castillo de Seboruco

Guantánamo

It is said that if it were not for the US naval base here and the famous song 'Guantánamera', this town would only be known to Cubans and music fans. The town itself was founded in 1796 to take in the French fleeing from revolution in Haiti. This has influenced the architecture, which is much less Spanish in style than in many other Cuban cities. It has narrow, brightly coloured buildings and thin balconies. The local music is also slightly different, with its origins in the coffee plantation culture of the 19th century.

The original sheet music for 'Guajira Guantánamera'

THE US NAVAL BASE

The American naval base at Guantánamo Bay was installed in 1903 as part of the Platt Amendment (1901), which was added to the new Cuban constitution by US Congress. This effectively made Cuba a protectorate of the USA, and gave the USA the right to have a naval base here. The Platt Amendment was repealed in 1934, but the lease on the base does not expire until 2033.

The existence of US territory on Cuban soil has fuelled much resentment against the USA even to this day. The $2,000 occupancy fee that the USA pays Cuba per year has been regularly returned to the USA since the Revolution. The base is effectively a remnant of the Cold War, with no military or political purpose other than a purely symbolic one. In the meantime, the USA spends many millions of dollars a year maintaining the base. In recent years, the USA has established detention centres on the base, housing several hundred terrorist suspects.

The US naval base is not far from the town, but has no impact upon life in the area. Visits can be made to the Mirador de Malones to view it through binoculars. Other than the naval base, there are few tourist sights in the town itself, although a walk around the well-restored town centre is pleasant.

Mirador los Malones

The US naval base is US territory in Cuba, granted by Cuba to the US Navy as part of the 1901 Platt Amendment. It covers 110sq km (40 sq miles) and is surrounded by 27km (16 miles) of fence. The base is not open to the public but can be viewed from a purpose-built viewing point (*mirador*), used by the Cuban authorities to spy upon the base. Tours start in an underground museum where a Cuban military attaché explains the history of the naval base and the current political issues. You can then go up to the top of the hill, where a telescope enables you to look at the base. Despite this being a military zone, you can film and take photographs.

MUSIC IN GUANTÁNAMO

The full name of the famous song is 'Guajira Guantánamera', written about a proud local girl with a habit of ignoring compliments paid to her. Its composer, Joseíto Fernández, wrote it in the 1940s, almost for fun. Later, verses from José Martí's poetry *Versos Sencillos* were adapted to the music. This song is used by virtually all music groups in Cuba as the climax to the show, and remains as popular as ever.

One of the main music styles in the area is *changüí*, a variation of *son* music that developed in the coffee plantations in the mountains. It utilises old-style bongos and an African thumb bass, and is regarded as one of the most complex but beautiful forms of *son*. The Tumba Francesa is a colourful folk dance tradition, as well as the name of a well-known music venue in Guantánamo. The folk dance was created during the 1890s by newly freed black slaves to preserve the cultural heritage that had been developed in the plantations.

24km (14¹/₂ miles) east of Guantánamo. The only way to view the base is by booking a tour in Santiago or in Hotel Guantánamo in the town. After entering the Cuban military zone, visitors travel for 10km (6 miles) through forests of cacti before reaching the viewing point.

Museo Provincial

This former prison now houses artefacts from the history of the province, including documents, photographs and memorabilia.
Plaza Martí, corner of Prado. Tel: 325872. Open: Tue–Sat 8am–12pm & 2–6pm, Mon 2–6pm. Admission charge.

Museo Zoológico de Piedra

This unusual open-air museum was founded by Angel Iñigo, a farmer and self-taught sculptor.

He has produced around 40 sculpted animals in stone, from tiny stone lizards to huge bison, all carved directly from the rocks in their natural setting. The location has a beautiful setting, surrounded by tropical vegetation.
Boquerón de Yateras. Open: Mon–Sat 9am–6pm. Admission charge.

The Casa de la Trova, Guantánamo

Driving tour: between Manzanillo and Marea del Portillo

This is a fascinating area of the island, with dramatic coastal scenery where the Sierra Maestra mountains almost fall into the sea along the south coast. The landscape is wild at times, and unspoilt by tourist development. The area is also important historically, and there are several interesting sites to visit. Most important among these is the Parque Nacional Desembarco del Granma, a park which commemorates the landing of the yacht *Granma* containing Fidel Castro's revolutionaries, which landed here in 1956.

Allow at least a whole day for this driving tour. For a more relaxed drive, visitors can choose to stay in Marea del Portillo, which is an excellent base for activities and excursions.
(See route on p140.)

The slopes of the Sierra Maestra

The tour starts in Manzanillo, a small seaside town with little interest in developing tourism. In fact, there are few dollar facilities and almost everything is paid for in pesos. Take the provincial road No 4, heading southwest from Manzanillo, and drive 10km (6 miles) into the hills.

1 Parque Nacional de Demajagua

It was here in 1868 that Carlos Manuel de Céspedes effectively started the first War of Independence by liberating his slaves. The ruins of this sugar mill in the hills were named after the bell that was used to call slaves to work, which became the symbol of opposition to Spanish colonial rule. The estate still has sugar-making equipment, including *calderas* for making molasses.

From here, continue along the same road for 40km (25 miles).

2 Media Luna

This small town was home to Celia Sánchez, a key figure at the beginning of the Revolution, who managed to get messages to different groups of revolutionaries when they were forced to scatter into the hills after the landing of *Granma* was met by Batista's troops. She later fought with Castro in the Sierra Maestra mountains and became his right-hand 'man' during the Revolution. She filled several important political positions after 1959 before dying of cancer in 1980. The house where she was born is now an interesting museum.

Continue for 23km (14 miles) along the same road (No 4), bearing right at the junction with provincial road No 20.

3 Niquero

The hotel in this village is a good place to stop for a drink or lunch. There are great views towards the sea, and of a sugar mill in the other direction, from the roof-top bar.

From Niquero, a dirt road takes you past Bélic to Las Coloradas. An alternative stop for food or drinks is Campismo Las Coloradas, a restaurant and group of huts just 4km (2 miles) southwest of Bélic.

4 Playa Las Coloradas

This is the historic heart of Parque Nacional Desembarco del Granma. For it is in a mangrove swamp just southwest of Playa Las Coloradas that

The replica of the yacht, *Granma*

Driving tour from Manzanillo to Marea del Portillo

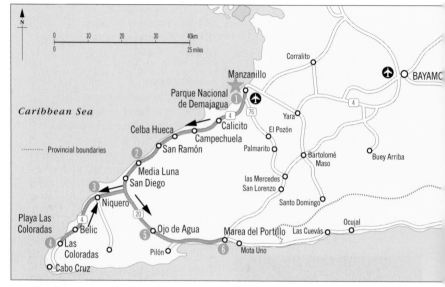

the yacht *Granma* landed with 82 revolutionaries on December 2, 1956. By the road there is a small park where a replica of the *Granma* can be seen. A 2-km (1-mile) concrete path through the swamp takes you to the actual site, now a concrete jetty with a plaque.

Rather than continue along this road to Cabo Cruz, and the tip of the peninsula, turn back past Niquero and turn right at the junction with road No 20, heading southeast towards Pilón.

5 Ojo de Agua

Before you reach Pilón you will see three separate signs and plaques marking the spots where the revolutionaries from the *Granma* crossed the road in underground water conduits, before heading into the Sierra Maestra. The signs have the

emblems of five palms in a heart, because the revolutionaries arranged to reassemble at a place called Cinco Palmas. *Once you pass Pilón, a sugar-producing town with a thriving commercial port, you continue east along the coastal road 15km (9 miles).*

6 Marea del Portillo

This stretch of the south coast contains the best beaches in the area. The scenery too is superb, with palm-trees and bays of volcanic sand at the foot of the mountains.

There are a few hotels here, plus an inlet surrounded by rocks and a beach of black sand. Some are all-inclusive hotels, which are popular with Canadian package tours, but most offer good facilities for water sports, diving, boat trips, hikes and horse rides.

View of the spectacular southern coast

Getting away from it all

The island is blessed not only with national beauty in abundance, but also government policy that develops tourist facilities in a carefully managed way so as to minimise the impact on the environment. While Cuba is internationally famous for its diving and sailing, nature lovers will find the island a paradise for hiking, birdwatching and other ecotourist activities.

Sailboats at Playa Pesquero

CYCLING

Cycling is increasingly popular, both as an activity to get away from the tourist centres, and as a means of seeing the island. It is a great way to enjoy the beautiful landscape and to get to know more of the real Cuba. Some travellers bring their bicycles to Cuba, while many tours and charity bike rides around the island, organised in the UK and elsewhere, take place during the cool season. Bicycles are available to rent from large hotels and holiday villages, and are generally of good quality, certainly much better than those used by the locals.

The country's infrastructure of roads is surprisingly extensive, and most of the country is accessible to cyclists. However, some of the roads are falling into disrepair, especially those in rural areas, and potholes are abundant. Traffic is generally light, particularly out of the main towns, and many Cubans have bicycles, because of the high cost of petrol.

If you are planning to cycle in Cuba, some preparation is essential. November to May is the best time of the year, when humidity is lower and tropical storms are infrequent. Cycling westwards is much easier, as there are strong year-round northeast winds. It is important to cycle only in the daytime, as roads are mainly unlit at night and can be dangerous.

In terms of where to go, there are many areas within striking distance of Havana, although the Sierra Maestra is a popular area with cycling tours. Cycling in Havana is a good way to see the city, although there is more traffic on the roads than before. Cruising the length of the Malecón is a must for foreign cyclists and locals alike, and there are some bicycle lanes and bicycle parking lots available. Out of the city, the Playas del Este can be reached on a day trip, while further out of the city, Soroa, Las Terrazas and Viñales are accessible, although there are some steep climbs and sharp bends.

Further information can be obtained from *www.cyclecuba.net, sales@havanatour.co.uk* and *trans@mail.infocom.etecsa.cu*

DIVING AND SNORKELLING

Cuba is one of the best places in the Caribbean for diving, due to its huge coastline (5,700km or 3,500 miles) and number of small islands (over 4,000), and also because of the pristine nature of its marine environment. The government has been proactive in protecting marine life, with the result that Cuba does not suffer the problems of overharvesting and overdevelopment in dive sites that have beset its Caribbean neighbours.

Due to the coral reef and offshore islands (*cayos*), there are no strong currents and visibility is often more than 40m (131ft). There are now about 15 zones developed for diving, with updated accommodation on site, and virtually every beach resort now has at least one dive centre. Both wall and platform dives are available along the coral reef, while there are a number of fascinating shipwrecks to explore, on account of Cuba's history of piracy and colonial trade.

The main dive areas are as follows:
Isla de la Juventud, south of the mainland. Cuba's most famous dive area, a marine park, is being established around the island by the government. The main centre is El Colony, while there are other good centres at Cayo Largo, at the eastern end of the archipelago.
María La Gorda, in the far west of the island. Great diving in a warm sheltered bay, with excellent visibility all year round.
Varadero, just east of Havana. One of the most developed areas for diving, with diving packages available. There are several sites around the offshore cays suitable for novice and advanced divers.
Archipiélago Jardin del Rey, on the north coast, north of Camagüey. There

Varadero is one of the best places to go diving

are two main dive areas in this large area. Santa Lucía has two dive shops and some fascinating historical wrecks, while Cayo Coco has beautifully clear water with large quantities of fish.
Santiago de Cuba area. There are two dive shops along the coast outside of the city: east of the city is Sigua Dive Centre (Carretera Baconao, 28km), while to the west is Sierra Mar (Playa Sevilla, Guamá).

There are also excellent dive sites in these other locations:
Faro de Luna, near Cienfuegos has over 18 reef sites and a variety of modern wrecks.
Jardines de la Reina, 80km (50 miles) south of the province of Camagüey. These islands have been declared a natural park and divers need an expensive licence to dive.

Playa Girón, near the Bay of Pigs.
There is a modern shipwreck here,
intentionally sunk by the government
for diving purposes.

Cayo Levisa, about 125km (78 miles)
from Havana, on the northwest coast.
The current is gentle, so this is an ideal
spot for beginners.

Guardalavaca, along the northeast
coast of the island in the province of
Holguín. There are two dive shops at
the resort hotels here. Lots of
underwater life, but not recommended
in the wet season.

HIKING

For hiking, the most developed areas
are in the Viñales area, the Topes de
Collantes area near Trinidad, and the
Sierra Maestra National Park. There are
regular tours from Trinidad around the
Topes de Collantes, and you can take a
refreshing dip in the natural pools here
(cars will not take you all the way; 4 × 4
jeep tours are recommended).

In the Sierra Maestra, a popular trek
is from Alto Naranjo to Las Cuevas.
There is also a challenging 5-km
(3-mile) hike from Santo Domingo,
the main base for the area, to the Alto
Naranjo viewpoint (950m or 3,120ft
high). Castro's forest HQ from the
Revolution can be visited too, with
a permit obtainable from the forest
rangers, a lovely hour's walk through
dense, often foggy forest.

Treks can be organised and guides
hired in Villa Santo Domingo, and
simple overnight accommodation is
available. The facilities are spartan and
some of the area is a military zone, so
not all areas are open to the public.

The Tocororo (Cuban Trogan)

HORSE RIDING

Trekking on horseback is also popular,
especially in the Viñales Valley. The only
riding centre in Havana is in Parque
Lenin, but in many ecotourist centres,
resorts and camping areas, horse-riding
facilities are available.

NATURE TOURISM

Nature lovers will find much to occupy
them on the island, as the Cuban
archipelago is home to a vast array
of flora and fauna, coupled with a
responsible and proactive ecotourist
policy from the government.

The island contains 6,700 species of
higher plants, half of which are endemic,
as well as 14,000 invertebrate species and
650 vertebrate species, including 350
species of bird.

Some jewels in the natural world
include the smallest frog in the world,
only 12mm ($\frac{1}{2}$ inch) long, as well

as the smallest bird in the world, the bee hummingbird (63mm/2$^1/_2$ inches). Cuba is home to 4 per cent of all the land species on the planet.

There are 116 nature trails to enjoy in Cuba, with a variety of landscapes. There are forests with unusual orchids, especially in West Cuba, dry mountainous areas with very old species of cactus, mangroves with tropical coastal ecosystems, wetlands with many biologically valuable species, and hummocks with rare fossil plants.

Ecotourist locations
Of particular interest to nature lovers is the Viñales Valley, declared part of the 'World Cultural Landscape' by UNESCO. It is internationally known for its beauty, the biodiversity of its vegetation and animal life, and it has the largest cave system in the West Indies.

The province of Pinar del Río also contains two biosphere reserves recognised by UNESCO: the Guanahacabibes peninsula in the far west of the island, and the Sierra de Rosario which includes Soroa, La Terrazas and the Santo Tomás cave system.

The Sierra de Rosario and Viñales Valley are within easy striking distance of Havana, and there are many tours available, either as day tours or where an overnight stay is possible (especially recommended if visiting the Viñales Valley). The Guanahacabibes peninsula can be reached by bus from Havana, with a change in Pinar del Río. Tours from Havana are popular, while there is more freedom of movement with a hired car.

Trekking in the Sierra de Escambray

Península de Zapata
The other main ecotourist area in Cuba is the Península de Zapata National Park and Biosphere Reserve which has a range of sites of interest: the Laguna del Tesoro, the Amerindian village of Guamá, La Boca crocodile breeding ground, and Playa Larga, to name the most important. This area is particularly suitable for birdwatchers, since the marshland ecosystem is a haven for hundreds of different species, including migratory birds. Among the 150 species of bird found in the Zapata Swamp, a UNESCO biosphere reserve, are the *zunzuncito*, the Cuban pygmy owl, a rare type of baldicoot called the Zapata rail, and waterhen. Manatees can be seen along the coast, while in the spring the beaches and roads are invaded by crabs leaving the water to mate.

The Península de Zapata can be visited by tours from Havana or

Horse riding in the Viñales Valley

Cienfuegos, and there are public buses on the Havana–Playa Girón route that stop in Playa Larga. However, a hired car is often more convenient in this area. It is well worth staying a few nights, especially for birdwatchers, who can be ready at dawn, before the tour buses arrive.

SAILING

The island is an ideal stopping-off point for yachts and sailing boats, and there are marinas offering moorings, boat rental and other services. The best time of the year for sailing is from December to April, when the weather is mild. However, the waters surrounding the island are generally calm, with plenty of bays.

The most popular area for sailing is the Archipiélago de los Canarreos, south of the mainland, and the biggest marina is the Marina Hemingway just west of Havana. The main marinas are owned by Cubanacán, Puertosol and Gaviota, which all offer a range of services, including excursions and boat hire.

Further information

A number of travel agencies organise specialist tours for nature lovers, the main one being Gaviota Tours: *Gaviota Tours, Edificio La Marina, Avenida del Puerto 102 between Jústiz and Obrapia, Havana. Tel: 666777.* For walking holidays in general, look at *www.ramblersholidays.co.uk*

Sailing boats at the Marina Hemingway, Havana

Shopping

There are a growing number of shops in Cuba, and the choice of goods has improved considerably in recent years. The main places to buy these are at the tourist centres where quality is high. The main items bought by visitors to take home include cigars, rum and handicrafts.

Stalls in the Mercato del Catedral

An Afro-Caribbean painting in the *Naif* style

State-run dollar shops, often situated in hotels, dominate the sale of souvenirs, but the legalisation of limited private enterprise has encouraged the growth of handicraft and food markets. These markets tend to have lower prices and bargaining is acceptable, compared to the higher-cost fixed-price state shops. Virtually all goods will need to be bought in US dollars. Cuba is good value compared with the rest of the Caribbean, but more expensive than Latin American countries.

Art

Art varies enormously in quality. One of the most popular styles is *Naïf* paintings, inspired by the Afro-Caribbean culture and often depicting landscapes and views of colonial towns. The Feria de Tacón near the Castillo de Real Fuerza in Havana is an excellent place to see the work of talented young artists. Bear in mind that you need documentation to take works of art out of the country, but galleries and even market vendors can give you the necessary stamp and paperwork.

Black coral

The black coral from Cuban reefs is famous as a material for making jewellery. Importing black coral and/or tortoiseshell into your home country is illegal as both are protected. While items may look stunning, do the oceans and your criminal record a favour and leave them in the shops.

Books and CDs

It's worth buying books and CDs in Cuba. Remember that CDs of music that is popular in Cuba are unlikely to be found outside the country. So if you want to be certain of owning a CD from Cuban musicians such as Los Van Van and Silvio Rodríguez, it's best to buy them while you're in Cuba.

Hand-made cigars on display for customers

Cigars

Cuban cigars are the best in the world, and make an ideal luxury gift, especially when packed in elegant cedar boxes. Do not be tempted to buy cigars from people soliciting on the street, as these are likely to be low-quality fakes. Make sure that the box has a branded label *hecho in Cuba totalmente a mano* (totally hand-made in Cuba), the official government seal, and the *Habanos* band.

You can only take 50 cigars out of the country without a receipt, but if you buy them in a state shop and get a valid receipt you can buy cigars up to the value of US$2,000 (except if you are travelling to the USA, where the importation of Cuban cigars is prohibited).

For more information, see the feature on Cigars on pp80–1.

Handicrafts

There is a huge range of unusual handicrafts available for sale in Cuba, made from raw material such as bamboo, shells, seeds, banana leaves and other plant fibres.

Medicines

It may come as a surprise to many visitors that Cuba is one of the leading producers and exporters of pharmaceuticals. Some of the medicines available include PPG, an anti-cholesterol drug obtained from sugar cane which is also good for arteriosclerosis, and shark cartilage which strengthens bones, especially good for children and older people. Food supplements include excellent honey, royal jelly and bee-glue (propolis), as well as spirulina which is derived from algae. International

pharmacies and duty-free shops in the airport are good places to buy pharmaceuticals.

Musical instruments

Many traditional Cuban musical instruments can be bought in music stores and markets. These include bongos, maracas, claves and tumbadora drums, which are played with the hands. Also popular is the *Güiro*, the gourd of the güiro fruit, which is stroked with a small stick.

Papier mâché

This technique is a relatively recent introduction in Cuba but is generating many high-quality goods. Brightly coloured masks, models of vintage cars, and toys can be seen in many markets.

Perfumes

The government-owned Suchel Camacho company produces very good perfumes, as well as face and body creams, all at good prices. Brands include the spicy Coral Negro, and the flower-scented Mariposa.

Rum

The most famous brand in Cuba is 'Havana Club', whose distillery can be visited in Havana. There are many types and prices for rum, mostly based on their age and quality. The most common type is 'Silver Dry', a young clear rum, while others are aged for seven years or more, and are more highly prized. Do not be tempted to buy sugar cane spirit or cheap firewater, as these may make you ill. *See the feature on Cuban Rum on pp52–3.*

Wood

There is a large range of very well-made wooden sculptures and figures on sale in markets and state-run shops. Many are inspired by African traditions, often using cedar and rosewood. Carved cedarwood cigar boxes are always crafted elegantly. Wooden objects can also be found on sale in the Galerías de Arte.

Where to shop

Havana

The capital has the best range of shops in the country, catering both for Cubans and tourists. However, shopping is not a leisure activity in Cuba, and the nearest you will get to this type of experience is at the big tourist hotels which have well-appointed, well-stocked shops. The shopping centres get very busy at weekends. The large department stores are mostly on Avenida Italia (Galliano),

between San Rafael and Neptuno.
Art: **Galería del Grabado** Original lithographs and other works of art can be purchased directly from the artists. *At the back of the 'Taller Experimental de Gráfica de la Habana', Callejón del Chorro 62, Plaza de la Catedral. Tel: 620979.*
Books: **Instituto Cubano del Libro** has three bookshops. *Palacio del Segundo Cabo, O'Reilly 4 and Tacón. Tel: 632244.*
Cigars: **Real Fábrica de Tabacos Partagás** This factory has a large shop selling a good range of cigars in lovely surroundings. *Industria, between Barcelona and Dragones (almost opposite the Capitolio).*
Food: **Isla de Cuba** has the best selection in Old Havana. *Máximo Gómez between Factoría and Suárez.* **Focsa Supermarket** has a good range of food. *Calle 17 between Calles M and N, Vedado.*

Roadside fruit stall, just outside Viñales

Handicrafts: **Palacio de la Artesanía**
A large selection of Cuban handicrafts,
as well as other items not available
elsewhere, such as footwear and
clothing. *Palacio Pedroso, Cuba 64,
between Peña Pobre and Cuarteles
(opposite Parque Anfiteatro). Tel: 671118.*
Music: **Artex** has a good selection of
music. *Calle L, corner of Calle 23.
Tel: 623228.*
Open-air markets: **Feria del Tacón** is
the city's largest craft market with a
huge range of products. *Avenida Tacón
between Chacón and Empedrado, very
near the Cathedral.* **Feria del Malecón** is
a busy market with lots of home-made
products. *Malecón, between Calles D
and E, Vedado.*
Photography: **Publifoto** develops films,
among other services. *Edificio Focsa,
Calle M, between Calles 17 and 19,
Vedado.* **Post Office**: sells film, floppy
disks and other photographic goods.
Plaza de la Revolución.
Shopping centres: **La Plaza Carlos
Tercera** A wide range of shops including
photography, cigars, sports and a
supermarket. *Avenida Salvador Allende,
between Arbol Seco and Retiro, Centro
Habana.* **Harris Brothers** Four floors
including fashion, childrens' clothes and
a supermarket. *Avenida de Bélgica 305,
between Paseo and Calle A, Vedado.
Tel: 553475.*
Other items: **La Maison** has dollar shops
selling cigars, handicrafts, jewellery, and
perfume. Also has fashion shows with
imported clothes. *Calle 16, 701 corner
of Calle 7, Miramar.* The **Caracol** chain
of shops in tourist hotels (*one in the
Habana Libre, Calle 23, Vedado*) sells
tourist goods as well as luxury items

such as chocolate, clothes, biscuits
and wine.

Santiago de Cuba

There is a good range of shops in this
city, many of which are around Parque
Céspedes. Handicrafts and books are
sold on the street on Heredia between
Hartmann and Pío Rosado.
Artex Music and videos. *Aguilera.*
La Bombonera A dollar store selling
food, very near Parque Céspedes.
Aguilera, between Lancret and Hartmann.
Casa de la Artesanía A good range of
hand-made products, including wooden
carvings and some lovely furniture.
*Under the cathedral in Parque Céspedes.
Tel: 623924.*
Librería Internacional A good selection
of books including paperbacks in
English. *Heredia, under the cathedral.*
La Maison Expensive European clothes,
dollars only. *Avenida Manduley.*
Photoservice Has several shops in town,
*including one on General Lacret under
the cathedral, another on Félix Peña
between Aguilera and Enramada.*
Salón Artexanda Sells arts and crafts.
*Heredia between Calvario and
Pío Rosado.*

Trinidad

There are not many shops in this small
colonial town, although they do cater
for tourists and offer a good selection
of handicrafts.
Bazar Trinidad sells handicrafts,
T-shirts, postcards and pictures. *Maceo
451, corner of Zerquera.*
Candonga (Mercado Popular de
Artesanía). The whole street at Calle
Toro is devoted to handicrafts, including

Embroidered linen at a market in Trinidad

contemporary art. *Villena 43, opposite Plaza Mayor.*

Galería de Arte Universal Sells contemporary Cuban art. *Villena 43, opposite Plaza Mayor.*

El Partón Sells food and drink, including ice cream and beer. *Hernández, next to Museo Romántico.*

Photoservice Photo services and goods. *José Martí, between Colón and Lino Pérez.*

Tienda Panamericana A dollar store selling clothes, food and toiletries. *Lino Pérez between Cadahía and José Martí.*

Universo A department store. *Martí, between Rosario and Colón.*

Entertainment

There is a wealth of entertainment options in Cuba, mostly centring around music. Out of all the islands in the Caribbean, Cuba is renowned for having the best nightlife, and it is hard not to get caught up in the intoxicating rhythms and hip-swaying movements that permeate the many local music venues in every city.

Salsa dancehall at the Hotel Melia Cohiba, Havana

Havana in particular has a range of options to suit all budgets. On many street corners, there will be music played and impromptu dancing, while in the tourist restaurants and bars groups of musicians come to play for a short while and gratefully receive any tips before moving on to the next location. Besides music, Cuba nurtures other forms of entertainment, from ballet and folk-dancing, to theatre, festivals and sporting activities.

Many Cuban airports have a small guide called *Bienvenidos a Cuba* which gives information on cultural events and shows, including addresses of venues. In Havana there is a free magazine *Cartelera* (www.cartelera.com) which details upcoming events, while other towns have leaflets or posters pinned up in strategic locations to let you know what is happening and when. Hotels are also good sources of information, with free leaflets and brochures.

Cinema

Cinema ticket prices are incredibly low, making it very popular with Cubans. Cuban cinema is called the 'seventh art' and the industry is thriving. There are

almost 200 cinemas in Havana, showing both Cuban and international films.

Havana: **Yara** – one of the largest in the city, but often sold out at weekends. *Opposite Hotel Habana. Tel: 329430. Libre, Vedado.* **Payret** – films shown continuously from 12.30pm. *Prado 503, corner of San José. Tel: 633163.*

Santiago de Cuba: **Cine Capitolio** – formerly a barracks in the uprising of 1956. *Victoriano Garzón 256.* **Cine Rex** – student members of the 1956 rebel forces were lodged here. *Aguilera 811, between Hernán Cortés and San Miguel.*

Trinidad: **Cine Romello Cornello** – Cuban and some American films. *On Parque Céspedes.*

Dance performances and lessons

It is relatively easy to get dance lessons; just ask at your hotel or *casa particular.* Displays of traditional folk or Afro-Cuban dance are sometimes given at music venues, but there are also specialist venues for dance.

Havana: **Casa de la Cultura de Plaza** – hosts concerts and shows, including traditional folk and *Santería* music, *Calzada and Calle 8, Vedado.* **Orestes Dickinson** – gives dance lessons.

The Casa de la Trova in Trinidad

San Lazaro 111, 1st Fl., Flat 3, between Crespo and Genios. Tel: 637359.

Santiago de Cuba: **Ballet Folkórico Cutatumba** – superb show on Sunday mornings. *Enramada, 2 blocks west of Parque Céspedes.* **Grupo Folklórico del Oriente** – lunchtime and evening shows. *San Francisco and San Félix.*

Trinidad: **Casa Fischer (Artex)** – has nightly shows of Afro-Cuban dance at 9.30pm. *Lino Pérez between Cadahía & José Martí.*

Nightclubs

There is a range of nightclubs offering different types of dancing and entertainment. Some are just discos, while others are much grander, offering a cabaret show and live music. Most start late at night with a smart dress code and under 18s are not usually admitted.

Havana: **Tropicana** – hosts perhaps the most famous cabaret shows in the Caribbean, with glamour and prices to match. It is best to go with a tour, bookable at most hotels and tourist offices. *Calle 72 No 4504 between 43 and 45, Marianao. Tel: 270110.*
Macumba – a top Havana disco with small floor show. *222 corner of 37, La Coronela, La Lisa (in La Giraldilla tourist*

The Casa de Tradiciones, Santiago de Cuba

complex). *Tel: 330568*. **Hotel cabarets** –
all the main hotels have their own shows,
some of which are the same standard as
the Tropicana and better value. *Hotel
Nacional, Riviera, and Habana Libre are
all recommended.* **Casa de la Musica** – a
great reputation with salsa disco and live
bands. *20 corner of 35, Miramar.
Tel: 240447.* **Tropical** – live salsa bands
most nights, with upper section and
popular outdoor location. *Salón Rosado
Beny Moré, Av 41 and 46. Tel: 290985.*

Santiago de Cuba: **Club Tropicana
Santiago** – considered one of the best
shows on the island. *Autopista Nacional
1.5km. Tel: 643036.* **Hotel discos** – some

hotels have lively discos, *including the
Santiago and Las Américas.*

Trinidad: **Casa de la Música** – daily
disco with live performers at weekends.
Plaza Mayor, up the steps past the church.
Las Cuevas – Merengue and salsa disco
in a cave nearby Las Cuevas Motel.
Finca Santa Ana. Tel: 4013.

Music and dance

Perhaps the most authentically Cuban
places for music and dance are the Casas
de la Trova which exist in all Cuban
towns. They vary from small,
unassuming venues which are mainly
frequented by locals, to full-blown

The Capitol and National Theatre, Havana

tourist venues. Most offer traditional live music, specialising in *son* and *bolero*. In some venues, especially the higher quality ones in cities, you will find Cubans desperate to get in, who will hassle you to pay their entrance fee. Locals will also be keen to dance with you, mostly for sociable reasons although don't be surprised if you find yourself buying the drinks all night!

There are also venues offering other types of Cuban music, including *rumba*, *conga* and *charanga*. There is a huge range of music and dance events happening in Havana. To find out more, look at the listings in the newspapers *Opciones* and *Cartelera*, which are found at most hotel reception desks each Thursday. In addition, Radio Fanio FM93.3 (an English and Spanish language tourist station) gives regular details of events.

Havana: **Casa de la Trova** – a small, intimate venue with traditional acoustic music, highly recommended, no bar. *San Lázaro between Belascoaín and Gervasio, Centro.* **Callejón de Hamel** – *rumba* show every Sun from noon. *Hamel between Aramburu and Hospital, Centro.* **Conjunto Folklórico Nacional de Cuba** – *rumba* and *santaria* music every Sat. *Calzada and 8, Vedado.*

El Delirio Habanero – quality music with great views. *Upstairs on 5th floor of Teatro Nacional, Vedado. Tel: 335713.* **Jardines 1830** – recently refurbished with top salsa bands playing. *Malecón and Calle 20 beside the road*

SANTIAGO FESTIVALS

There are quite a few festivals in Santiago over the summer. The 'Festival de Baile' takes place May 15–19; the 'Festival de Caribe' starts first week in July and continues into late July. The Carnival itself is from July 18–27. Festivals also take place Sept–Dec, including a huge party on New Year's Eve.

tunnel. Tel: 334521. **Jazz Café** – live jazz every night, recommended, on top floor of blue glass building. *Galerías de Paseo, Primera between Calles A and Paseo, Vedado.* **La Zorra y el Cuervo** – recommended venue for jazz and salsa,

The electrifying carnival atmosphere in Santiago

with entrance through a British red phone box! *Calle 23 and O, Vedado. Tel: 662402.*

Santiago de Cuba: **Casa de las Tradiciones** – colonial house with loads of atmosphere, good for both listening to live music and for dancing. *Rabí between José de Diego and García.* **Casa de la Trova** – very popular but touristy upstairs venue overlooking the street. *Heredia 206.* **Casa de los Estudiantes** – a popular venue, in a beautiful building with a patio where bands play. Check in advance what shows are planned. *Heredia, very near Hotel Casa Granda.* **Grupo Folklórico del Oriente** – day and evening dance performances by folk groups. *San Francisco and San Félix.*

Trinidad: **Casa de la Trova** – good Cuban music in delightful open-air terrace. *One block southeast from the church, just off Plaza Mayor.* Near the Casa de La Trova, you will come across several music venues. Just follow your ear. Most are pretty good. **La Canchánchara** – serves a tasty drink of the same name in earthenware pots, and has traditional music at lunchtimes. *Villena 70.* **La Escalinita** – balmy terrace to the right of the church, up the steps, with live music at lunchtimes and evenings.

Theatre and ballet

The most important venues for theatre, classical music and ballet are all in Havana. There are many festivals held in Havana: see the Festivals section on *p30* for more information.

Teatro Nacional de Cuba – a complex which holds several auditoriums, hosting all kinds of cultural events and

Poster for the Ballet Nacional de Cuba

arts festivals. *Paseo corner of 39, Vedado. Tel: 8796011.* **Gran Teatro de la Habana** – Cuban National Ballet and Opera, and Conjunto Folklórico Nacional perform here. *Prado, corner of San Rafael, Centro Habana. Tel: 8613078.* **Amadeo Roldán** – marvellously renovated concert hall in which the national and visiting symphony orchestras play. *Calzada & D, Vedado. Tel: 321168.*

Children

Children will have a great time in Cuba, not only because there are a lot of sights of interest and activities suitable for them, but also because Cubans love children and you will be treated very well as a result. The family is very important in Cuba and you will soon make conversation everywhere you go.

The beach near Trinidad

Beaches
Beaches are the obvious starting point for families, and there are many lovely beaches, such as Cayo Coco which has shallow, warm water for many metres out to sea. Beach resorts such as Varadero and Guardalavaca are ideal for children, as there are excellent facilities for water sports and for organised activities.

Cities and excursions
Havana is good for children, particularly Habana Vieja, around the Plaza de Armas. There are regular displays of dancing and other activities in the Museo de la Ciudad. The Castillo del Morro and fortification of San Carlos de la Cabaña are also fascinating historical sites which children will enjoy.

They will also appreciate the range of transport options in Havana – after all, how many children from Europe or North America have travelled in a *bicitaxi*, *cocotaxi*, horse-drawn *coche*, or a 1950s Chevrolet?

Excursions from Havana are plentiful, with a variety of tours to the beautiful countryside. The tour to Las Terrazas takes you to an ecological community

and natural springs where visitors can swim. A trip to the Viñales Valley should not be missed, either. Learning how tobacco, sugar cane and coffee are grown will fascinate most children.

In Trinidad, there are excursions to nearby Playa Ancón, or a ride on the old steam train that takes you through Valle de los Ingenios to the Iznaga estate tower and farmhouse, where there is a sugar cane press that produces a refreshing juice.

Nature parks
Cuba has developed its wildlife reserves and ecological sites very carefully, with the result that there are many sights where nature and wildlife can be enjoyed. Nature parks include:

Jardín Botánico Soledad, Cienfuegos: a serene and fascinating botanical garden which includes massive Banyan fig trees and an impressive collection of cacti.

Parque Baconao: this is the largest amusement park in Cuba, with a range of attractions that are ideal for children. One can climb up the enormous monolith of Gran Piedra, take a boat trip on Laguna Baconao, spend hours at the children's park of Valle de la Prehistoria with its dinosaur sculptures, visit the excellent aquarium which has regular dolphin shows, and watch rodeo shows at El Oasis. There are also coffee plantations and beaches.

Península de Zapata: the area around Laguna del Tesoro is particularly rich in wildlife and includes the holiday resort of Guamá with its thatched huts, as well as an excellent crocodile farm.

The Valle de la Prehistoria in Parque Baconao

Sport and leisure

Sport plays an important part in life on the island, both for tourists and locals. There is a wide range of outdoor leisure activities available to tourists, such as diving, fishing and sailing. For those who like to watch rather than participate, baseball is the prime spectator sport in Cuba, although there are other options available too.

Kayaking at Caya Coco beach

PARTICIPATORY SPORTS AND LEISURE ACTIVITIES

Caving

There are a number of huge cave systems in Cuba, some of which have been developed for tourists, while others are known only to professional cavers. The main sites are:

Camagüey – Sierra de Cubitas has several caves containing Amerindian pictographs, such as Los Generales, Las Mercedes, Indio and Pichardo.

Gibara – Tanques Azules, Caletones. The adventure park at Silla de Gibara offers activities such as potholing and cave diving.

Isla de la Juventud – Cuevas del Punta del Este also contains Amerindian pictographs.

Trinidad – Cueva Martín Infierno contains the largest stalagmite in Cuba.

Viñales – Santo Tomás and Cueva del Indio caves.

Zapata peninsula – there are flooded caves here, which can be dived.

Cycling

Cycling is a great way to see Cuba, as

there is an excellent network of tarmac and concrete roads, making most of the country accessible to cyclists. Traffic on the roads is very light, especially out of the main towns, and the scenery can be spectacular. A lot of the roads are in poor condition, with large potholes, but there are plenty of roadside workshops (*talleres*) where repairs can be undertaken.

Some of the bigger hotels and holiday villages have good-quality bicycles for hire, but bear in mind that these will be far superior to the ones that the locals have, many of which were imported from China, so always lock your bike or leave it in a supervised place.

November to May is the best time for cycling in Cuba, and it's best to try to cycle from east to west, in order to avoid the strong northeast trade winds.

For more information, contact:
Blazing Saddles Travels (*www.cyclecuba.net*) or **Havanatour UK** (*www.havanatour.co.uk*).

Diving

Cuba is one of the best places in the Caribbean for diving, due to its huge coastline (5,700km/3,500 miles), the

Preparing for a dive

quantity of small islands (some 4,000), and the pristine nature of the marine environment.

The main dive areas are: Isla de la Juventud, María La Gorda, Varadero, Archipiélago Jardin del Rey, and the Santiago de Cuba area.

Further information on diving in

Cuba can be obtained from:
Cubanacán Nautica, *Calle 184 No 123, Reparto Flores, Havana. Tel: 336675.* The main company that owns the dive shops (as joint ventures with the Cuban government) is:
Cubanacán (*www.cubanacan.cu*),
See the Getting Away From It All

Locals fishing on the Malecón

section (p142) for more information on diving.

Fishing

Ernest Hemingway is credited with popularising fishing in Cuba, and deservedly so. Both excellent deep-sea and freshwater fishing are available.

For freshwater fishing, the *trucha* (largemouth bass) is the most popular fish to catch. Deep-sea fishing can be organised at most marinas around the island, although the best facilities are at Marina Hemingway, west of Havana.

Marina Hemingway *Ave 5 and 248, Santa Fé, Playa, Havana. Tel: 241150.*
Havanatur Pesca y Caza *Edificio Sierra Maestra, Calle 1 between 0 and 2, Playa, Havana. Tel: 247541.*

Golf

Cuba currently only has two golf courses, although ten more are being built in many of the tourist areas.

Golf at a course in Boyeros (towards Havana airport)

The nine-hole Golf Club in Havana welcomes non-members and costs $30–40 for two rounds. Equipment can be hired and lessons are available. The entrance fee of around $5 includes use of the other sporting facilities: swimming pool, squash and tennis courts, billiards and a bowling alley.

Club de Golf Habana – *Carretera de Vento km 8, Capdevila, Boyeros (towards the airport). Tel: 338918.*

The Varadero golf club has been upgraded in recent years from 9 holes to 18 holes, the original course being laid out around the mansion of the family Dupont, now the *Xanadú Club House*, built in the 1920s. The facilities are good, with putting greens, a chipping green and a driving range, as well as lessons and hire equipment offered. Packages of a few days are available with accommodation in the clubhouse. **Club de Golf Las Américas** – *Avenida las Américas, Varadero. Tel: 668442. Open daily, make reservations 24 hours in advance, through tour desks or direct with the club.*

Horse riding

Horse riding is a popular activity for travellers wanting to spend time in the countryside, especially in the Viñales Valley. In many ecotourist centres, resorts and camping areas, there are horse-riding facilities available.

There is a riding centre in Havana. It costs around $5 per hour with guide included. There is no need to reserve, just turn up. The centre is well run and horses are well looked after. **El Rodeo** – *Parque Lenín (near the Las Ruinas restaurant), Havana.*

Hunting

The country has a number of hunting reserves (*cotos de caza*) where people are allowed to hunt birds and small animals under the supervision of forest rangers. Many lodges for freshwater fishing also have hunting facilities. There are no specialist hunting agencies but more information can be obtained from **Havanatur Pesca y Caza** *Edificio Sierra Maestra, Calle 1 between 0 and 2, Playa, Havana. Tel: 247541.*

Sailing

The island is an ideal stopping-off point for yachts and sailing boats, and there are marinas offering moorings, boat rental and other services. Most sailing is done around the Archipiélago de los Canarreos, while the best time of the year for sailing is from December to April, when the weather is mild.

The biggest marina is the **Marina Hemingway** *Ave 5 and 248, Santa Fe, Playa, Havana. Tel: 241150.* **Puertosol** owns many of the tourist marinas: *Calle 1 3001 corner of 30, Miramar, Havana. Tel: 245923.*

SPECTATOR SPORTS

Baseball and boxing are by far the most popular sports in Cuba, but volleyball, basketball, athletics and football are also widespread. After the Revolution, professional sports were abolished and big investments were made in amateur sports and in physical education in general. Cuba has some outstanding teams, particularly in baseball, boxing, volleyball, athletics, weightlifting and water polo. For more information on sports in Cuba, contact **Cubadeportes SA** *Calle 20 No 710, between 7 and 9, Playa, Havana. Tel: 240945.*

The main venue for watching sports in Cuba is the Ciudad Deportiva ('Sports City') in Havana. It is enclosed by a dome and seats 18,000 spectators, being built in 1958. It hosts a wide range of sports, from volleyball and basketball, to martial arts and table tennis. International sporting events are usually sold out. Attending is highly recommended due to the great

atmosphere and cheap entrance fee, only a few Cuban pesos. There are limited food and drink facilities, so remember to take your own.
Ave. Rancho Boyeros and Vía Blanca, Havana. Tel: 545000. Buy tickets at the venue in advance.

The following stadiums also regularly host sporting competitions:
Estadio Panamericano *Carretera de Cojimar 1.5km, just outside Havana. Tel: 974140.* Swimming, water polo, football, athletics and baseball.
Sala Polivalente Ramón Fonst *Ave Rancho Boyeros and Bruzón, Havana. Tel: 820000.* Volleyball and basketball.

Baseball
Cubans have a great passion for their national game, which first developed in the late 19th century as a symbol of national identity and anti-colonialism. The official baseball season is from November to March, culminating in the national play-offs. There are regular games on some weekday evenings and at weekends. Games can last up to three hours although this doesn't seem to dull the spectators' fanaticism! Tickets for games cost a few pesos and can be purchased at the stadium box office just before the game. The best place to see major league baseball is the Estadio Panamericano. Built in the 1950s, it is home to two teams, the Industriales (Los

Azules) and Metropolitanos, and seats 55,000 spectators.

Boxing
Cuba has one of the best boxing teams in the world, winning many Olympic titles. Fights can be seen in Havana at **Sala Kid Chocolate**, *Paseo de Martí and Brasil, Havana (opposite the Capitolio). Tel: 611546.* This used to be the only venue in Havana where fights could be viewed. It has recently been converted into a bar.

Cycling
Havana's professional racetrack is at the Velódromo Reinaldo Paseiro, part of the Estadio Panamericano, on the south side of the Vía Blanca. Cuba hosts several international competitions, including *Vuelta a Cuba* in February. For more information, contact the **Federación Cubana de Ciclismo** in Habana del Este. *Tel: 973776.*

Renting a bicycle is inexpensive and fun

Food and drink

The quality and range of food in Cuba have improved a great deal in recent years, and there is much more fresh produce available. However, visitors expecting new culinary experiences and haute cuisine will be disappointed. Drinking in Cuba, however, is a highly pleasurable experience, with rum taking centre stage on the alcoholic front, and with a range of fruit juices and other packaged drinks available, too.

Inside a restaurant

What to eat

Traditional Cuban food is known as *cocina criolla* and is based on a mixture of Spanish, African and Colombian Indian influences. It is rarely spicy. The national dish is roast pork with *congrís* (rice mixed with black beans) and yuca (cassava) or fried plantain. Main dishes mainly consist of rice and beans with either chicken or pork, with a salad of tomatoes and cucumber. Fish and seafood is good, too, and readily available to tourists. The main soup,

Typical tourist fare

potaje, is made from black or red beans, garlic, onion, pepper, powdered cumin and pork. Another soup is *ajiaco*, a kind of minestrone made with a variety of vegetables and meat. The choice for vegetarians is unfortunately very limited, although pizzas, salads, omelettes and cheese sandwiches are available, but be aware that beans and rice are often cooked in meat fat. However, with advance warning, your restaurant or *casa particular* will prepare proper vegetarian food.

There is a magnificent range of fresh fruit, and, depending on the season, mango, guava, papaya and pineapple are available. Visitors from the UK in particular will notice the fantastic flavour that fresh fruit and vegetables have in Cuba, compared to those at home.

Cubans are big fans of ice cream, and there are often queues at ice cream parlours, especially at *Coppelia*.

What to drink

Rum is the national drink and forms the basis of all cocktails. There is a huge range available (*see the feature on Cuban Rum on pp52–3*).

Beer is pretty good, the most common brand being Cristal, a light beer, and Bucanero, stronger and very popular in Santiago de Cuba. Hatuey beer is also available, especially in Havana. Cuba does produce wine, but it is not particularly good. Imported wines, especially from Chile, are a better bet.

There is a large range of delicious fresh fruit drinks available, as well as shakes (called *batidos*), using fresh papaya, mango, pineapple and oranges. The most common fruit squash is lemonade, made with lime, sugar, water and ice. Also recommended is *guarapo*, made from fresh sugar cane (it isn't as sweet as you might think!). Packaged soft drinks are available in cans, bottles or cartons. Canned soft drinks are called *refrescos*, while fruit juices can be bought in cartons and are very popular. Try the *Guayaba*-flavoured one if you want something a little different.

Cuban coffee is very strong and not to everyone's taste. It is often sold in tiny cups and sometimes has sugar already added. Teas are also available, especially camomile (*manzanilla*).

Where to eat

The standard and choice of dishes are much higher in international-class hotels than in state-run restaurants. One of the advantages of staying in *casas particulares* is that the home-cooking is often excellent, with huge portions, and your hosts are often able to buy all sorts of ingredients in private or black markets. They may or may not have government licences to serve food to their guests.

A fast-food restaurant

State-owned 'dollar' restaurants vary hugely in quality, but some may be quite good. Do not expect authentic dishes if you eat at restaurants offering international cuisine. Resort hotels tend to offer buffet meals as part of the 'all-inclusive' package, and these can sometimes get tedious, although breakfasts are normally excellent.

Private restaurants are called *paladares* and often consist of a handful of tables with a limited range of dishes. It is impossible to recommend particular *paladares* because they open and shut so frequently, depending on the government's policy at the time for giving out licences. Visitors are often approached in the street and offered to be shown to a *paladar*, which may or may not have the required government licence: if you take them up on their offer, note that they will receive a commission from the *paladar*.

If you want snacks or fast food, these are available in the streets of most towns. Small pizzas are normally filling and good value. There is an American-style fast-food chain El Rápido, which offers a safe but bland bet for many people.

In the restaurant listings below, star ratings indicate the average cost of a meal per person, excluding drinks.

★   Less than $10
★★ $10–25
★★★ $25–45
★★★★   over $45

HAVANA

Havana has the biggest choice of restaurants with the highest quality and quantity of ingredients, and costs are higher than in other cities as a result.

Al Medina ★
Arab food in lovely colonial mansion.
Oficios between Obrapía and Obispo, Habana Vieja. Tel: 671041.

Dominica ★★★
Very smart Italian restaurant with vegetarian options.
O'Reilly, corner of Mercaderes, Habana Vieja. Tel: 602918.

Floridita ★★★
Sumptuous décor, and another favourite haunt of Hemingway (the stool in the corner of the bar is kept empty in his honour).
Corner of Obispo and Monserrate, next to Parque Central, Habana Vieja. Tel: 671299.

La Paella ★★
The best paella in Havana, in a charming setting.
Monserrate, between Obispo and Obrapía, Habana Vieja.

El Tocororo ★★★★
Excellent food including ostrich steak, in colonial

mansion with terrace.
Calle 18 and Av 3. Tel: 242209.

La Torre ★★★
Best French food in Havana, with great views.
Calles 17 and M, at top of Edificio Fosca, Vedado. Tel: 325650.

SANTIAGO DE CUBA

Santiago 1900 ★★★
Famous restaurant in former residence of Bacardi family.
Calle Massó 354. Tel: 623507.

Steak House Toro de Santiago ★★
Meat dominates the menu, some reputedly imported from Canada.
Avenida de las Américas, corner of Cebreco. Tel: 642 011.

La Taberna de Dolores ★★
Good value Spanish food.
Aguilera, corner of Reloj. Tel: 623913.

Terrazas ★★
Good food on the upper floor.
Calle 5 50 between M and Terraza. Tel: 642491.

TRINIDAD

Don Antonio ★★
Good Creole restaurant, with fish a speciality.
Calle Izquierdo 118 between Bolívar and Guinart. Tel: 3198.

The Tocororo, Miramar, Havana

There are many high-quality restaurants in Havana

El Jigüe ★★
Good food and atmosphere, often with live music.
Maceo 402, corner of Colón. Tel: 4316.

Plaza Mayor ★★
Elegant setting with buffet dinner available.
Villena 15, just of Plaza Mayor.

Sol y Son ★★
Pleasant 19th-century house with courtyard. Includes vegetarian options.
Simón Bolívar 283, between País and Martí.

Where to drink
Most bars in Cuba have live music of one sort or another. Most will be visited by groups of musicians who play for 15 minutes and then gather tips and try to sell their CDs before moving

on to the next venue. Music venues in contrast will have a more structured evening of music. We have detailed only the best or most popular bars in the major cities.

HAVANA
Bar El Louvre
A great place at street level to watch the sun going down over Parque Central.
At Hotel Inglaterra, Prado 416. Tel: 608595.

La Bodeguita del Medio
Perhaps the most popular with tourists in Havana, because of its links to Hemingway. Always crowded.
Empedrado 207, just by the cathedral.

Casa de la Amistad
Peaceful, with a beautiful garden extension.

Paseo 406, Vedado. Tel: 303114.

Havana Café
A very popular 1950s theme place.
Entrance to the left of main entrance of Hotel Meliá Cohiba, Paseo between Calles 1 and 3. Tel: 333636.

Hotel Sevilla
Nice courtyard with fountain. Popular with Graham Greene fans.
Trocadero 55 and Prado. Tel: 608560.

SANTIAGO DE CUBA
Baturro
Bar with nice atmosphere, specialises in *Rocío del Gallo*, made with coffee and rum.

Las Columnitas
Outdoor bar and café.
One block from Enramada, San Félix and Callejón del Carmen.

TRINIDAD
Bar Las Ruinas de Segarte
Pleasant bar in ruined courtyard.
Alameda between Márquez and Galdós.

Bodequita de Trinidad:
Music bar with courtyard and quaint sheltered booths for couples.
Colón between Martí and Maceo.

Hotels and accommodation

There is an increasing choice of accommodation in Cuba, and standards have risen dramatically since 1980 when the country opened its doors to foreign visitors. While Cuba is focusing much of its efforts to attract the package-holiday tourist to its beach resorts, as well as upmarket tourists to its cities, there is still much available for other types of traveller.

The Melia Cohiba Hotel, Havana

Casas particulares

The most authentic and rewarding place to stay is in a *casa particular*, private accommodation often offered by Cuban families who rent one or more spare rooms in their home. This type of accommodation has been available since 1996 when the government allowed the renting of private rooms to those who registered and paid the relevant taxes. Not only is this option better value than hotels, it also facilitates contact with locals in a friendly and informal environment, giving visitors a chance to learn much more about everyday Cuban life than they could otherwise do. *Casas particulares* are often spotlessly clean, with great hospitality and sometimes with home-cooked meals available. These houses are recognisable by the stickers on

A *casa particular* in Havana

front doors containing two blue chevrons on a white background, with '*Arrendador Inscripto*' written on it.

Hotels

The hotel sector is growing quickly, with all hotels being owned by the government, some of which are partly owned by foreign partners in joint ventures. The best hotels are those with foreign management or foreign investment, and most have 4 or 5 stars. There are some mid-range, Cuban-owned hotels built in the 1950s, but they are often run-down and below international standards. Some old historic buildings have been refurbished into beautiful hotels, and are well worth a visit.

There are a large number of hotel chains in Cuba. Gran Caribe is the most upmarket, while the other high-quality chains are Cubanacán and Sol Meliá. Horizontes hotels are of a slightly lower standard, while Islazul is more basic. Some old buildings have been converted into lovely hotels and shops by the Habaguanex chain in Havana.

It is important to book your first night's accommodation well in advance of travelling, especially during the peak season of December to February. Visitors will need to fill in a hotel name and address on their Tourist Card before travelling to Cuba, otherwise this may cause delays or problems on arrival.

Price guides

The price categories below will give you a rough idea of the kind of accommodation in each price range:

$100+   These are international standard hotels, mostly joint ventures with foreign management. Some of the more modern ones may lack an authentic feel and could be anywhere in the world. Others are located in historic buildings, in which case they may have sumptuous interiors and lots of charm.

$60–100   Hotels in this category will be very high quality, with good facilities and furnishings. Some may be small, intimate and charming.

$30–60   This is the lower end of the state hotel sector, and hotels in this price category are less likely to have been recently renovated. Fixtures and fittings may well be outdated and the hotel may have a shabby atmosphere, especially in the cities. In the countryside, these hotels may be much more attractive.

Up to $30   For this budget, it is highly recommended to stay in *casas particulares* rather than hotels, which are likely to be low quality and well below the standard that many tourists would find acceptable. *Casas particulares*, on the other hand, are likely to be clean, hospitable and comfortable.

A typical all-inclusive hotel resort in Varadero

Hotel visits

There are some famous hotels, particularly in Havana, that have been restored to their former glory, and which are well worth visiting to admire the décor and charm, and to enjoy a drink or meal. Although some are way beyond the budget of most travellers, some have lovely bars or restaurants in sumptuous settings which are well worth a diversion. Below is a recommended selection of historic Havana hotels:

Ambos Mundos: made famous by Hemingway, with a charming 1930s feel. *Calle Obispo 153, corner of Mercaderes.*

Hostal Conde de Villanueva: converted 17th-century mansion. *Mercaderes 202, corner of Lamparilla.*

Hotel Inglaterra: famous historic hotel with Spanish-style foyer. *Paseo de Marti 416, between San Rafael and San Miguel.*

Nacional de Cuba: Havana's most prestigious hotel, with 1930s atmosphere, and lovely gardens. *Calle O, corner of Calle 21, Vedado.*

Santa Isabel: splendid colonial building facing the Plaza de Armas. *Baratillo 9, between Obispo and Narciso.*

Practical guide

The José Martí airport in Havana

Arrival

Formalities

The requirements and documents asked for by the Cuban immigration authorities are a valid passport, a return ticket, and a Tourist Card (*tarjeta de turista*). Tourist Cards are valid for 30 days and are solely for visits of a tourist nature. They can be issued by the travel agency or airline from whom you bought your air ticket, or a Cuban consulate. You will need to fill in your personal data and where you are planning to stay in Cuba (often the name of the hotel where you are staying on your first night). Tourist Cards can be extended for another 30 days by going to the Immigration Office in Havana.

Special regulations apply for holders of US passports. American law makes it illegal for US passport holders to travel to Cuba, but it is possible to obtain a licence from the US Treasury Department if the trip is for religious or humanitarian trips or for freelance journalists or university students. Some US travellers visit Cuba by travelling via Canada, Mexico or the Caribbean and not having their passport stamped by the Cuban authorities.

Visitors for non-tourist reasons such as business people, journalists, students, and nationals of countries without a visa-free agreement with Cuba, should check visa requirements. An official/business visa may be required.

By air

Havana is the main international airport in Cuba, although there are several

A Varadero beach

others classed as international, including Varadero. The international terminal at Havana airport includes shops, exchange facilities, snack bars and so on. Immigration can be slow, especially at night. There are no hotels at the airport, so visitors will need to take a taxi to the city, which will cost $15–25. There is an accommodation desk at the airport if you need to book a last-minute hotel.

Camping

There are official campsites all over Cuba, although they are mainly used by Cubans on holiday. They mostly consist of basic cabins, although some are designed for tourists with campervans. The main agency to arrange bookings and transport for camping is *Cubamar, based in Havana at Paseo 306 between 13 and 15, Vedado.* In addition, each major town will have a *Campismo* office for access to local campsites.

Children

Children should experience no real problems in Cuba, but sensible precautions should be taken. The sun is very strong, so protection in the form of a hat and strong sunscreen are required,

and lots of bottled water should be drunk. Remember to take a supply of toilet paper, as public toilets are generally hard to find and often very dirty. Wet wipes and antiseptic hand cream are also very useful.

The most common health problems for children are diarrhoea and vomiting. To avoid this, it is best to avoid ice in drinks, and food or drinks sold on the street. The treatment of diarrhoea is the same as for adults but should start earlier and be more intensive.

Climate

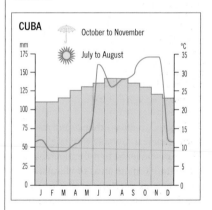

CUBA — October to November — July to August

Weather Conversion Chart
25.4mm = 1 inch
°F = 1.8 × °C + 32

Cuba has a moderate subtropical climate, due to its location under the Tropic of Cancer, with warm temperatures and an average of 330 days of sun per year. There are two seasons: the rainy season (May to October) and the dry season (November to April). The summer months of June to September are warmer and sunnier than the rest of the year, with average summer temperatures of 25°C (77°F). A winter average is 22°C (71.6°F). The day and night temperatures differ less in the coastal regions than they do inland.

Due to its long and narrow shape on an east–west axis, Cuba experiences refreshing trade winds and sea breezes. Santiago de Cuba on the southeast corner is the exception to this, being several degrees warmer than the rest of the island. The eastern part of the country is generally warmer than the west. The water temperature is usually around 25°C (77°F).

Conversion tables
Clothing sizes are usually given in US or European measurements, depending on the origin of the item. *See p183.*

Crime
Compared to most other countries in Latin America, Cuba is very safe. Travellers will find that they are able to walk around most areas of Havana and other cities at any time of the day, without feeling ill at ease. Punishments for crimes against tourists are severe. However, the level of petty crime is increasing, mainly due to the growing number of tourists on the island and the large financial gains available, and there have been reported cases of robberies, especially pick-pocketing or bag snatching. Remember, Cuba is a poor country where the average salary is about $10 per month.

Leave your valuables, documents and money in the hotel safe. Do not carry all your money with you in the same place.

If carrying a day-rucksack, hold it in front of you when in crowded places, especially bars. Take some of your money as travellers' cheques (not American Express). Do not wear showy jewellery or have your camera too visible. If you hire a car, park near hotels or in pay car parks wherever possible, and do not leave any belongings visible in the car.

Customs regulations
You are allowed to take into Cuba items whose overall value is no more than $250, plus medicines up to a maximum weight of 10kg (22lb). It is forbidden to import fresh food or plants, as well as explosives, drugs or pornographic material.

In terms of duty-free allowances, you can bring in a maximum of 200 cigarettes or 50 cigars or 250g (9oz) of loose tobacco, and 3l (0.66 gallons) of wine or other alcoholic beverages, provided that you are over 18.

If you intend to take more than 50 cigars out of the country you must produce a receipt of their purchase at a state-run shop. To take works of art out of the country you must have an official stamp, available from most art shops and stalls.

Avoid buying items made from protected or endangered species such as tortoiseshell, black coral or bags or belts made from non-farmed reptile skins. These are covered under the Convention on International Trade in Endangered Species (CITES).

Driving
Travelling by Car
Travelling by car is an excellent way to see the island, especially out of the

Queuing for a bus, Havana

major cities. Roads will be relatively empty, although traffic is increasing as the economy picks up. The condition of the roads is variable, although *autopistas* are mostly fairly good. Towns often have a lot of potholes in the streets. It is best to keep your speed down, even on *autopistas* as there are often slow-moving vehicles on the road.

In the summer, it is best to drive in the mornings to avoid the hottest part of the day. Many Cubans hitch-hike and a lift will be appreciated, although you are not obliged to pick up hitch-hikers. It is not advisable to travel at night, as lighting is very poor and there will be people and animals walking on the road. Signposting is mostly very poor, so you may well need to ask for directions in many areas.

Car hire

Car hire is relatively expensive, especially when adding in the cost of petrol, although it is an increasingly popular way to see the island, and fly-drive packages are available from abroad. To hire a car while in Cuba, tourists must have a driver's licence from their home country or an international licence, be over 21 years of age and be able to show their passport to the car rental company. The main companies include Transautos and Havanautos which have good support networks, and many airports and large hotels will have a car rental desk. Try to ensure that the car is filled with fuel to avoid having to search for a petrol station on your first day.

1950s taxis in Havana are intended for locals only

Fuel

Petrol is available to foreigners in *Cupet* stations, payable in dollars. There are not many stations outside the main towns, so it is best to fill up wherever possible, well before the tank gets empty. Many car-hire companies will be able to give you a free copy of an *automapa* which shows locations of stations across the island.

Parking

Park in supervised car parks or near hotels wherever possible. Thefts of wheels from hire cars or belongings from cars are not uncommon.

Traffic regulations

In Cuba, traffic drives on the right. The speed limit is 20km/h (12mph) in parking areas, 50km/h (31mph) in towns, 60km/h (37mph) on dirt roads, 90km/h (56mph) on asphalt roads and 100km/h (62mph) on *autopistas*. Seat belts are often only fitted on more modern cars and are not compulsory. In general, the police are fairly tolerant with tourists. It is common practice to sound the horn when overtaking a lorry or before making a sharp turn.

Electricity

The electricity supply is 110 or 220 volts AC, 60 Hz, with flat-pinned plug sockets. Many recently-built hotels have 220-volt currents, but the most usual is 110 volts (same as in the USA). For visitors with European-style appliances, it is a good idea to buy a voltage converter before travelling.

Embassies
Canada
No 518, Calle 30, corner of Av 7,
Miramar, Havana.
Tel: 2042516.
United Kingdom and Northern Ireland
No 702–4, Calle 34, corner of Av 7,
Miramar, Havana.
Tel: 2041771.
US Interests Section
Calle Calzada between L & M, Vedado,
Havana.
Tel: 333551 or 333554.

Emergency telephone numbers
Ambulance and First Aid: *Havana*
405093; Santiago 226185.
Police: *Havana 867777; Santiago 226116.*
Fire Brigade: *Havana 867555; Santiago*
226115.

Health
Cuba should pose no unusual health
risks: the country has an excellent
health system and there are not many
tropical diseases, meaning that no
vaccinations or inoculations are
required. Visitors travelling in rural
areas in rough conditions may wish to
consider vaccinations for typhoid, polio,
tetanus and Hepatitus A. Insect repellant
is recommended, especially if you are
visiting wetlands or swamp areas.
However, everyday pharmaceutical items
are in short supply so it is best to bring
your own supply of pain relievers,
antibiotics, stomach treatments and
so on.

Around 95 per cent of hotels have a
doctor on the premises for the provision
of primary care to patients. In addition,
there are eight international clinics that

offer specialist treatment in Pinar del Río,
Varadero, Cienfuegos, Trinidad, Cayo
Coco, Santa Lucía, Guardalavaca and
Santiago de Cuba. Payment is in dollars,
and medicines can be bought here.

Health regulations are only applicable
to travellers from countries where there
is endemic yellow fever and cholera, or
countries declared infected areas by the
WHO, in which case an International
Vaccination Certificate is required. It is
advisable for all tourists travelling to
Cuba to take out health insurance.

The most common health problem in
Cuba is diarrhoea and vomiting, caused
by stomach bugs or food poisoning, and
the usual treatments of rest, fluid and

Cuban mineral water is safe and widely available

LANGUAGE

BASIC		NUMBERS	
hello	hola	0	cero
goodbye	adiós	1	uno (m), una (f)
yes	sí	2	dos
no	no	3	tres
friend	amigo (m), amiga (f)	4	cuatro
thank you	gracias	5	cinco
Where is the bathroom?	¿Dónde está el baño?	6	seis
		7	siete
COURTESY		8	ocho
please	por favor	9	nueve
thank you	gracias	10	diez
you're welcome	de nada	20	veinte
sorry	disculpe	30	treinta
excuse me	perdon	40	cuarenta
it doesn't matter	no importa	50	cincuenta
		60	sesenta
GREETINGS		70	setenta
How are you?	¿Cómo estás?	80	ochenta
Very well, thank you	Muy bien, gracias	90	noventa
Good day, good morning	Buenos días	100	cien
Good afternoon	Buenas tardes	200	doscientos
Good night	Buenas noches	300	trescientos
How's it going?	¿Cómo te va?	400	cuatrocientos
What's happening?	¿Qué pasa?	500	quinientos
What's your name?	¿Cómo te llamas?	600	seiscientos
Welcome	Bienvenido	700	setecientos
		800	ochocientos
CHANGING MONEY		900	novecientos
Where can I change dollars?	¿Dónde puedo cambiar dólares?	1000	mil
travellers' cheques	cheques de viajero		
Is the bank open?	¿El banco está abierto?		
How much is the dollar worth?	¿A cómo está el dólar?		
Do you need identification?	¿Necesita identificación?		
Where do I sign?	¿Dónde firmo?		
May I have some large and small bills?	¿Puede darme billets grandes y chicos?		
the rest in change?	¿el resto en cambio?		

APPROACHING SOMEONE FOR HELP

excuse me, sir	perdón, señor
ma'am	señora
miss/ms	señorita
Do you speak English?	¿Habla usted inglés?
I'm sorry	Lo siento
I don't speak Spanish	No hablo español
Please speak more slowly	Hable más despacio, por favor
please repeat	repita, por favor
May I ask a question?	¿Una pregunta, por favor?
Could you please help me?	¿Podría ayudarme?
Where is ...?	¿Dónde está ...?
thank you very much	muchas gracias

PAYING THE BILL

The bill, please	La cuenta, por favor
How much do I owe you?	¿Cuánto le debo?
Is service included?	¿El servicio está incluido?
This is for you	Esto es para usted

EATING

bread	pan
butter	mantequilla
coffee	café
fork	tenedor
knife	cuchillo
napkin	servilleta
pepper	pimienta
plate	plato
salt	sal
spoon	cuchara
tea	te
water	agua

DAYS OF THE WEEK

Sunday	domingo
Monday	unes
Tuesday	martes
Wednesday	miércoles
Thursday	jueves
Friday	viernes
Saturday	sábado

MONTHS OF THE YEAR

January	enero
February	febrero
March	marzo
April	abril
May	mayo
June	junio
July	julio
August	agosto
September	septiembre
October	octubre
November	noviembre
December	diciembre

DIRECTIONS

left	izquierda
right	derecha
far	lejos
near	cerca
street	calle
avenue	avenida
north	norte
south	sur
east	este
west	oeste

salt replacement are recommended.
To avoid these problems, it is best to
avoid ice in drinks, and food or
drinks sold on the street. Cuba is
relatively humid, so visitors are likely
to feel tired and apathetic for the
first few days. Remember to drink
lots of bottled water; avoid the
tap water.

Insurance

Make sure you have adequate travel
insurance before you travel, and always
read the small print. All losses must be
reported to the police and/or hotel
authorities within 24 hours and a
written report obtained for insurance
purposes. This may be difficult to obtain
but necessary.

When hiring a car, two optional
insurances are available. The first
covers accidents but not theft, and the
second covers all risks except for the
loss of a tyre. In the event of an
accident, a copy of the police report
must be obtained to show the car-hire
company.

Internet

Internet access is increasingly available to
foreigners in Cuba, although very few
Cubans are allowed access to the web. Pre-
paid cards are available from the ETECSA
phone company which allow access for a
set number of hours. The main locations
for internet access in Havana are the
Capitolio and the International Press
Centre in Vedado (*Calle 23*). Major hotels
also have internet access but these tend to
be more expensive. Other major tourist
towns in Cuba tend to have at least one
internet café.

Lost property

To report the loss or theft of personal
documents or belongings, go to the
nearest police station or find a police
officer. You may have to wait a long
time to make your report. Remember
to take a photocopy of the main sections
of your passport, in case you lose the
original.

Maps

Maps are usually very good in Cuba
and more up to date than those
bought abroad. One of the
recommended maps is the *Mapa
Geográfico* (Ediciones GEO). The
best map for drivers is the *Guía de
Carreteras* (Road Guide), which is
very accurate. Maps can be bought
at tourist offices and major hotels,
and in Havana a good shop for maps
is the Instituto Hidrográfico, *Mercaderes
between Obispo and Oficios*.

Media

The leading daily newspaper in Cuba
is *Granma,* which has a weekly
international version published in
English, French, Portuguese and Spanish
called *Granma International*. Internet
versions can be found at *www.granma.cu*.
There is a business monthly paper on
investments in Cuba, *Business Tips on
Cuba.*

There are two national TV channels,
Cuba visión and Tele Rebelde, while
there are several national, municipal
and regional radio stations. Many
hotels have a satellite dish with CNN
in Spanish or English, and some
broadcast a TV channel especially
for tourists.

Money matters
Currency

The Cuban peso is the national currency. There are notes of 1, 3, 5, 10, 20, 50 and 100 pesos, as well as coins equivalent to 1 and 3 pesos. There are coins of 1, 2, 5 and 20 cents.

Most products available to tourists are paid for in US dollars. A recent ban on the dollar enacted by Castro in retaliation against increased trade restrictions imposed by the USA is, however, making the dollar less important than it once was. Out of the city centres, small goods such as chocolates or sandwiches are paid for in Cuban pesos. It is always useful to have a very small amount of pesos.

Besides the US dollar and the Cuban peso, the tourist will find a third currency in circulation: the Convertible Peso (Peso Convertible). These banknotes are accepted everywhere without question and exchanged at par with the US dollar. Most cash-machines issue only Convertible Pesos whereas banks generally provide US dollars or a mix of both. Two warnings, however: be careful not to confuse the Convertible Cuban Peso (the word 'convertible' is clearly written on the front of the note) with the Cuban peso (moneta nacional) which is worth far less: the Convertible Peso is not exchangeable outside Cuba, so make sure you have none left in your wallet when getting onto the plane to fly back home.

In 1996, Cubans were allowed to hold US dollars for the first time. Many Cubans are desperate to earn them, so that they can buy goods in shops such as clothes and shoes, and white goods such

Conversion Table

FROM	TO	MULTIPLY BY
Inches	Centimetres	2.54
Feet	Metres	0.3048
Yards	Metres	0.9144
Miles	Kilometres	1.6090
Acres	Hectares	0.4047
Gallons	Litres	4.5460
Ounces	Grams	28.35
Pounds	Grams	453.6
Pounds	Kilograms	0.4536
Tons	Tonnes	1.0160

To convert back, for example from centimetres to inches, divide by the number in the third column.

Men's Suits

UK		36	38	40	42	44	46	48
Rest of Europe	46	48	50	52	54	56	58
USA		36	38	40	42	44	46	48

Dress Sizes

UK		8	10	12	14	16	18
France	36	38	40	42	44	46
Italy	38	40	42	44	46	48
Rest of Europe	34	36	38	40	42	44
USA		6	8	10	12	14	16

Men's Shirts

UK	14	14.5	15	15.5	16	16.5	17
Rest of Europe	36	37	38	39/40	41	42	43
USA	14	14.5	15	15.5	16	16.5	17

Men's Shoes

UK	7	7.5	8.5		9.5	10.5	11
Rest of Europe	41	42	43	44	45	46
USA	8	8.5	9.5	10.5	11.5	12

Women's Shoes

UK	4.5	5	5.5	6	6.5	7
Rest of Europe	38	38	39	39	40	41
USA	6	6.5	7	7.5	8	8.5

as washing machines that are often only sold for dollars. Holding US dollars is now against the law for locals, however, a black market in American currency continues to thrive.

Exchange

It is best to arrive in Cuba with US dollars, both in the form of cash and travellers' cheques. Remember that credit cards or travellers' cheques issued in the USA (mainly American Express) will not be accepted in Cuba.

Banks are usually open from 8am to 3pm, Monday to Friday. Exchange offices are mostly open 24 hours a day. Services include cashing travellers' cheques and withdrawing money over the counter using a credit card (but not an ATM card). Some tourists use exchange facilities at their hotel but the commission is often higher.

Cuban police officers are generally helpful and courteous

Credit cards

All hotels and many restaurants and shops will accept payment by credit card, as long as it is not issued in the USA. Any problems using credit cards should be reported to the Centro de Tarjetas de Crédito in Havana. However, it is important to carry a certain amount of cash to pay for smaller purchases.

Opening hours

Normal working hours on weekdays are 8am to 5.30pm. Banks generally are open from 8am to 3pm. Museums tend to open between 10am and 5pm Monday to Friday, and Sunday morning only. However, they have been known to close at unpredictable times, so it may be a good idea to phone ahead.

Police

Police officers in Cuba have a reputation for helpfulness and politeness, and rarely trouble foreigners. The main type of police are the PNR (Policía Nacional Revolucionaria), with light blue shirts and dark blue trousers. There are also tourist police who often speak English and who wear dark blue uniforms.

Post offices

The Cuban postal service is not the most reliable or the fastest, although it is comparable to other Latin American countries. Stamps (*sellos*) can be bought in hotels or post offices (*oficinas de correo*). The fastest way to send important letters or parcels is via international courier services such as DHL, Cubapost or Cubapack.

Public holidays

January 1 Liberation Day. Anniversary of the Triumph of the Revolution.
May 1 International Workers' Day.
July 25, 26 and 27 Festivities in honour of the July 26, 1953 attack on Moncada Garrison.
October 10 Beginning of the Wars of Independence.

Public transport

Getting around the island is relatively easy and there are a number of options available. For those with limited time and more money, flying is the quickest way of covering the long distances on the island. There is a good network of internal flights, and flights can be booked at most travel agencies at reasonable cost.

For up-to-date details of long-distance bus, ferry and rail services consult the *Thomas Cook Overseas Timetable* published six times a year. It is available to buy online at *www.thomascookpublishing.com* or from branches of Thomas Cook in the UK (*tel: 01733 416477*).

The next best option is long-distance buses. The best service is Víazul, although Astro also offers a reasonable service. Coaches are relatively comfortable for long journeys and tend to be fairly punctual. They often have toilets and reclining seats, but the down side is that they often play low-quality videos and are often very cold due to the strong air-conditioning. Distances are large, though; for example, Havana to Trinidad is a 5- or 6-hour journey.

Trains are best suited for people with time on their hands and limited

A *camello* (camel bus) used by Cubans only

budget. Breakdowns and long delays are commonplace, while the level of comfort and facilities are not high. The most popular route is between Havana and Santiago de Cuba, and tickets can be obtained from the Ferrotur offices in Havana.

Travelling by sea is also possible, the most used routes being between Havana and Isla de la Juventud, and Havana and Varadero.

In towns, public transport is available in the form of buses. Due to fuel shortages, long articulated lorries are used, called *camellos* (camels) due to their shape. Buses are very cheap but almost always crowded and uncomfortable, and not for tourists.

Sustainable tourism

Thomas Cook is a strong advocate of ethical and fairly traded tourism and believes that the travel experience should be as good for the places visited as it is for the people who visit them. That's why we firmly support The Travel Foundation: a charity that develops solutions to help improve and protect holiday destinations, their environment, traditions and culture. To find out what you can do to make a positive difference to the places you travel to and the people who live there, please visit *www.thetravelfoundation.org.uk*

Telephones

Run by ETECSA, the phone network is improving but is still not very efficient. New phones enable the use of pre-paid phone cards (*tarjetas telefónicas*), which can be bought at hotels, shops and ETECSA phone centres.

If you are calling Cuba, dial the international access code (e.g. *00* in the UK), then the country code for Cuba (*53*) followed by the local area code and

An ETECSA Telephone Centre in Vedado, Havana

Tipping is recommended in restaurants

phone number. The number of digits in local phone numbers varies according to the size of the town.

For private phones, international calls must be made through an operator and will always be reverse charge.

Phone codes in Cuba

From abroad: *00-53* – area code – number
From Cuba: *119* – country code – number
For direct dialing (*teleseleccion*): *0* – area code – number
These are the main regional codes. All codes refer to provinces unless otherwise indicated.
Camaguey *32*
Cayo Largo *45*
Cienfuegos town *432*
Cienfuegos province *33*
Granma *23*
Guantánamo *21*
Havana city *7*

Havana province *64*
Holguin *24*
Isla de la Juventud *46*
Las Tunas *31*
Matanzas *45*
Pinar del Rio province *8*
Pinar del Rio town *82*
Sancti Spiritus *42*
Santiago de Cuba *22*
Trinidad town *419*
Varadero *45*
Villa Clara *42*
Zapata peninsula *45*
Directory enquiries *113*
Operator *00*
International operator for reverse charge calls *09*
To make a direct-dial international call from a public phone *119*, plus the international access code:
Australia *61*
Canada and USA *1*
New Zealand *64*
UK *44*

Time

Cuba is five hours behind GMT (Greenwich Mean Time), like the US east coast. In the summer there is daylight saving time, the same as in Europe.

Tipping

Tipping is recommended in hotels and restaurants, if only a small amount (a dollar or two for a US$25 meal). Cubans who work in the tourist industry tend to pool their tips to be shared between all staff. No tip is expected for food or accommodation at *casas particulares*, but musicians in bars or restaurants always expect to receive a donation for playing.

Toilets

Toilets are pretty basic, especially in public places where they are often filthy. It is a good idea to carry toilet paper with you wherever you go, as it is generally not supplied. Wet wipes or antiseptic hand cream are also worth carrying.

In most places, toilet paper is placed in the rubbish bin rather than in the toilet, due to the poor state of the sewage system.

Tourist information

Tourist information on Cuba can be found in the following countries.

Canada (Montreal)
440 Bd René Levesque Ouest, Suite 1105, PQ H2Z 1V7, Montreal.
Tel: 1-514-8758004; fax: 1-514-8758006;
www.gocuba.ca

Canada (Toronto)
55 Queen St, East Suite 705, M5C-1R6 Toronto.
Tel: 1-416-3620700; fax: 1-416-3626799;
www.gocuba.ca

United Kingdom
154 Shaftesbury Avenue (first floor), London, WC2H 8JT.
Tel: 44-207-2406655;
fax: 44-207-8369265; tourism@cubasi.info

Within Cuba, there are tourist desks in most hotels, such as Rumbos, Horizontes or Cubanacán, which offer tours, transport or accommodation. In Havana, there is a small network of tourist information offices, called *Infotur*, which sell maps. Several can be found in Calle Obispo in Habana Vieja. The Ministry of Tourism is at *Calle 19 710, between Paseo & A, Vedado, Havana. Tel: 334318.*
Useful information can also be obtained through these websites:
www.cubatravel.cu; www.infotur.cu; www.dtcuba.com; www.cubaweb.cu and *www.islagrande.cu*

Travellers with disabilities

There are few facilities for people with disabilities. It is not easy to get around in towns, due to the high pavements and many potholes and loose paving stones. Some of the newer hotels in Varadero have some rooms adapted for wheelchair use, but most of the older hotels in Cuba, as well as *casas particulares*, have no facilities. It is recommended to do some research in advance and to book with a good tour company. One agency that caters for tourists with specific needs is Cubanacán Turismo y Salud (*www.cubanacan.cu/ingles/index.html*).

What to take

There are items that are in very short supply or unavailable in Cuba, which are

A *cocotaxi*, used by tourists

advisable to take not only for your personal use, but also for use as gifts.

In terms of what to wear, light and casual clothing is most suitable. As in other latin countries, there is a clear distinction between male and female attire, and traditional attitudes prevail for the most part. A warm layer is useful, especially on long-distance buses where the air-conditioning is very strong. A waterproof is handy due to occasional tropical rainstorms.

Medicine is very expensive and scarce in Cuba, so bring all the medicines that you may need. Include items such as painkillers, indigestion pills, anti-diarrhoea preparations and rehydration salts, antibiotics and a first aid kit.

You should also bring items according to your individual circumstances such as insect repellent, razor blades, toilet paper, wetwipes, antiseptic hand-cream, condoms, tampons, disposable nappies,

camera film and accessories, a torch and batteries, sun protection (high factor sun cream, glasses and a hat), and reading and writing materials.

Suitable gifts that will be gratefully received by Cubans include all of the above, as well as vitamin pills, sewing needles, magazines and CDs or cassettes of western music (unavailable on the island). Some travellers take old clothes and shoes to wear while in Cuba, and donate them before returning home. Many Cubans cannot afford to buy new shoes or clothes, so any gifts (especially foreign goods) are welcomed.

However, it is advisable not to give gifts to locals or children in the street who ask for them, as this merely encourages further hassling of tourists. It is best to donate to Cubans who you know or organisations that can distribute any gifts judiciously.